THE ULTIMATE BOOK OF MEMORY ALBUMS

- 205 album page examples

- 8 easy-to-do lettering styles

- hints, tips and techniques

The Album Page Designers

We are grateful to the following people for creating the 205 album pages which appear in this book. Some of these designers work for manufacturers who supply products for memory albums, and some have scrapbooking retail stores (see page 144). We're proud to feature their cute, pretty, charming and gorgeous album pages. In alphabetical order, they are:

- Janye Anderson for Sonburn
- Gina Barker for Gussie's
- Barbara Barnes for All Night Media, Inc.
- Brenda Birrell for Pebbles in My Pocket
- Channa Brewer for Memory Lane
- Anne Cook for The Gifted Line®
- Brenda Cosgrove for Pebbles in My Pocket
- Eileen Davis for Provo Craft®
- Sandi Genovese for Ellison® Craft & Design
- LeNae Gerig for Hot Off The Press
- Becky Goughnour for Hot Off The Press
- Dee Gruenig for Posh Impressions
- Wes Heaps for Provo Craft®
- Joy Hulsh for Pebbles in My Pocket
- Stacy Julian for Paper Hearts
- Sharon Lewis for Memory Lane
- Kim McCrary for Pebbles in My Pocket
- Allison Myers for Memory Lane
- Sonia Paulsen for Memory Lane
- Monica Schmidt for Memory Lane
- Bridgette Server for Memories & More™
- Ann Smith for Memory Lane
- Anne-Marie Spencer for Hot Off The Press
- Julie Woolley for Paper Hearts

Hot Off The Press Production Credits:

Project editors:	Mary Margaret Hite
	Tara Choate
	Katie Hacker
Technical editor:	LeNae Gerig
Photographer:	Kevin Laubacher
Graphic designers:	Sally Clarke
	Jacie Pete
	Susan Shea
Digital imagers:	Michael Kincaid
	Larry Seith
Editors:	Paulette Jarvey
	Tom Muir

published by  P.O. Box 55595
Little Rock, Arkansas 72215

produced by

Canby, Oregon USA

ISBN 1-57486-092-5

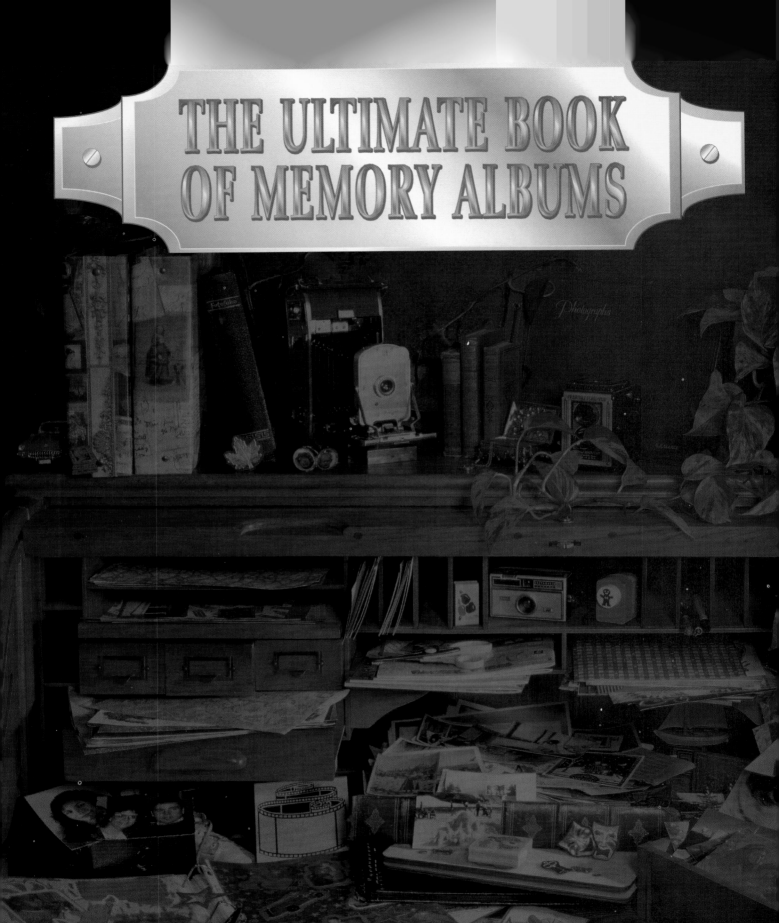

THE ULTIMATE BOOK
OF MEMORY ALBUMS

Table ~of~ Contents

Introduction

What are memory albums all about? Our personal photos are important, but they're often stored in shoe boxes. Here's how to easily get them into albums to be seen and shared.

Tools

Scissors, stencils, rulers and templates are the basic ingredients. We'll cover them all with easy and fun ways to create great album pages.

Papers

Patterned and plain papers are essentials for memory albums. With them you can spend an hour on a page, or just minutes. We'll show you how! Plus ideas using neon, velour and metallic papers and even paper doilies.

Stationery

Stationery is easy to use and easy to find. These bordered papers are perfect to frame a portrait or highlight one prized photo on an album page. But here are other creative uses for stationery.

Stickers

What could be easier—just peel and stick! Stickers are everywhere and found in every theme imaginable. Just be sure yours are acid-free. Here are some of the best and most creative ways to use them.

Punches

Punches are evolving from simple shapes like circles and squares to intricate corner treatments and elaborate shapes. All the latest are shown with unique uses to easily embellish your pages.

Die Cuts

Die cuts are paper shapes cut with a machine. They provide easy, inexpensive decorative elements for album pages. Stores have die-cut machines for their customers to use, or die cuts packaged by theme.

Rubber Stamping

Memory album pages provide a great place to use rubber stamps. It's easy to stamp a border, background, photo frames, or to do embossing.

Decorative Extras

Anything goes in this chapter! There are album pages using computer clip art, paper crimpers, rub-ons, doilies, die-cut photo corners and even fabric.

Journaling

The final touch to your album pages, and perhaps the most important. Here are lettering styles from plain to fancy. Use them on all your pages, or just for titling.

Keepsakes

These album pages show how to incorporate many of those precious mementos—locks of hair, kids' artwork, wedding and graduation announcements, newspaper clippings, diplomas, ribbons and more!

Black & White Photos

Here are many ways to beautifully mount both sepia-toned and black-and-white photos. You'll even learn how to easily color tint these photos.

Introduction

Photography has been part of our lives since 1839 when the first photograph, a copper-plate "daguerrotype" was revealed to the world. Since then we have experienced "Kodak moments" or remembered the times of our lives. We've grabbed Polaroid cameras to give us instant gratification, or underwater and panoramic cameras to offer more options for fun photos. But what to we do with these 16 million unique photos we take each year? Why, they're in shoe boxes tucked under beds and in forgotten closets all around the nation. Ouch!

There is a rumbling going on and it's all about Memory Albums, also known as Scrapbooking. It has to do with people gathering their photographs, cutting them and gluing them onto decorative papers, perhaps embellished with stickers or die cuts, then doing something called "journaling." There are parties of (mostly) women meeting to work on their creative albums. We've even heard of all-night cropping events. What's this all about? How can it be *new* when I remember making an album as a youngster?

Obviously the activity of creating an album or scrapbook isn't new; however, now there are new tools to make the process more fun and creative. More importantly, there seems to be renewed interest in preserving our history. As society "cocoons" and feathers its nests, we begin to focus on our families and their histories. It could be because the baby boomers are reaching their 50's and coming to an understanding that they are mortal. But that doesn't account for the enthusiastic 14-year-old boy searching for the perfect paper for his album, or the college-age young women who are working on their own albums, or the young mothers carving out time to keep their family albums up to date. Even some schools offer classes on albums in which the students create their own album stories. Perhaps that's it—we each have a unique story to tell and, even if you're not good with words, you have tons of pictures each "worth a thousand words."

We know that, heaven forbid, if our house were on fire and all the living occupants were safe, the loss of our precious photos would bring tears to our eyes. They are irreplaceable and so dear, yet they remain in attics and basements gathering dust.

Where to start? Be kind to yourself and begin with your most recent photos. Chances are you'll know where they were taken and remember the names of everyone in each photo. Then, as you are able, work back in time to organize photos of the past by the date or event. If you try to start with your birth or marriage, the task will soon become overwhelming, and you'll push those shoe boxes back in the closet and miss out on all the fun!

What's to know? Acid-free is the watchword in this activity. Items so labeled have a neutral pH and will not cause your photos to deteriorate any faster than nature allows. Use only acid-free papers, glues, stickers, die cuts, pens, sheet protectors—well, you get the idea. There are pH pens which can be used to tell you the acidic content of unlabeled products. With this activity becoming so popular, manufacturers are racing to determine the acidity of their products and to so label them.

What's important? Keep the activity fun. Don't spend two hours creating the perfect album page unless you have that kind of time. Perhaps you'll embellish only half your album pages. Helpful hint: Use a sheet of patterned paper (the kind with all over designs) as the background paper and you don't need to do much embellishing. Remember, just like in kindergarten, this is paper, scissors and glue. Don't drive yourself crazy. Keep it manageable so you'll continue saving those memories!

This book is divided into chapters by product. We'll begin with an overview of memory albums and show examples of cropping. Then we'll explore each of eight product categories with album pages using those products—tools, papers, stationery, stickers, punches, die cuts, decorative extras, and rubber stamps. Finally we'll discover journaling, how to use keepsake items and what to do with black-and-white photos.

We do have one caution: Making memory albums is addictive! You may want to make an album for each child (or have them help on their own books) or make a smaller album dedicated to a special vacation or one exclusively for Christmases. Also an album is a uniquely wonderful gift. We invite you to join us in an extremely satisfying activity that will be treasured for years to come by you yourself and by those you love. Best of all, you possess all that is necessary—photos and a caring for the memories of your life.

What must I have? In making memory albums you'll use paper, scissors and glue—yes, as in kindergarten. Here's a list of the very basics:

Acid-free adhesive: Stick glue, liquid glue, double-stick adhesive sheets or squares, corner mounts, or tape runners (with pieces of double-stick tape on a roll)—just be sure the label says acid-free.

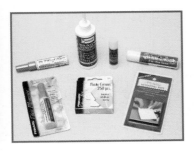

Plain papers are available by the sheet, in packages by color assortment or in book form. They need to be acid-free and lignin-free.

Acid-free black pen: Many widths are available; a medium tip, .03 or .05, is a good all-purpose size.

Album or binder: There are lots of choices and at least two sizes. Since most papers are 8½"x11", a binder of this size works well. 3-ring binders allow you to easily add or rearrange pages. Do NOT use "magnetic" albums, which may not have acid-free sheets and can destroy photos. Be sure all interior sheets are acid-free, lignin-free.

Straight scissors

Pattern-edged scissors: It's great to have one or more pattern-edged styles. You can add other designs as you create album pages.

Patterned papers, like plain papers, are sold individually, in packages, or in books by theme. They must be acid-free and lignin-free, too.

Templates: To begin it's best to have a few basic templates with several sizes of circles, ovals, hearts and stars. Some templates have a decorative ruler on the edge.

Sheet protectors typically come to fit 8½"x11" pages; however, 12"x12" are coming onto the market. They can be top-loading or side-loading. Be sure they are acid-free—never use any made of vinyl.

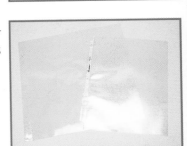

What's nice to have?

As you create album pages, you may want to add to your tool box with a wider selection of the must-have items listed above—more pattern-edged scissors, templates and papers. As you go through the chapters of this book you'll find lots of "nice-to-haves." They include die cuts, stickers, punches, a corrugator (also called a paper crimper or tube wringer), red-eye pen (to remove the red glare in flash photos), pet-eye pen (to remove the glare from animals' eyes), patterned rulers, stencils, pH pen (to test acidity), doilies, rubber stamps, colored pens and more. New products are appearing on the market everyday, so you'll never be bored!

9

1

3

5

7

2

4

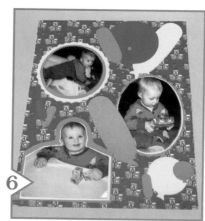

6

Page Construction

Here are the basic steps to creating an album page. You'll need the "must haves" listed on page 9.

1 Select your photos for one album page based on a theme, event or some common thread.

2 Select the papers to complement your photos.

3 Cut the photos (called cropping—more of this on the next page). Here is where you'll use those patterned-edged scissors and templates.

4 Mat the photos with plain or patterned paper. This is easy—just glue the cut photo to your chosen mat paper and trim ⅛"–½" outside the photo with straight or patterned scissors. You can make single, double or triple mats, or even more—whatever you like.

5 Arrange the photos on the page. You don't have to cover every square inch.

6 Add decorative elements—die cuts, punches, stickers, doilies, rubber stamps, etc. There will be tons of ideas in the pages of this book.

7 Write a description of the person, action or events shown in the photos. This is called "journaling" and is very important in order to make your album a book of memories, rather than just a collection of photographs. Write directly on the album page or onto a piece of paper which is then glued to the page. You can journal in your own handwriting, with a computer or typewriter, press-on letters, stickers or other aids. Many people dislike their handwriting, but journaling is important to add. More about this on pages 110–121.

8 Slip the finished album page into an acid-free sheet protector, then into your album or binder. Many sheet protectors fit 8½"x11" papers, but 12"x12" sheet protectors are coming into the market.

Cropping

By cutting ("cropping") photos to show only the most important parts you'll be able to get more photos on a page, and they'll be more interesting. If you are unsure about cropping, make color copies and practice on those. It's really easy! **Tip:** When cutting, it's easier to turn the photo than the scissors.

1 Trim close to the focal person or thing. Use straight or pattern-edged scissors.

2 Leave historical items like houses, cars or furniture—they'll be fun to see years from now.

3 Use a plastic template for perfect circles, ovals and smooth shapes. Position the template over the photo and mark with a pen or a grease pencil. Cut inside the line.

4 For another look, cut a silhouette by trimming close to the focal person or thing. Don't worry, you don't have to cut perfectly. It's a great look!

5 It's fun to "bump" out a part of the photo with your scissors—look at this bunny's ears and the baby's feet. Some other "bump-able" examples are balloons, elbows, hats—there are many examples in the photos in this book.

6 **Cropping Polaroid photos:** Older photos (8–10 years old) may separate when cut from their white bindings, but this isn't harmful to them (or to you). If you include part of the white seam just above the writing plaque, the photo is less likely to separate. Newer photos taken on Spectra film do not separate so easily; however, years of bending on flexible album pages might cause separation. You can use the same cropping technique for them, or the pieces can be held together with a sheet protector. Before cropping a just-taken Polaroid, wait 10–15 minutes after it develops so it is completely dry. Never cut into the white envelope at the bottom of the photo—this is where the developer is located.

7 If you are hesitant to cut one-of-a-kind photos, make color copies (even if they are black-and-white photos) and crop these.

8 Mat your photos (see page 10). Mix straight scissor cuts with pattern-edged cuts for a variety of looks.

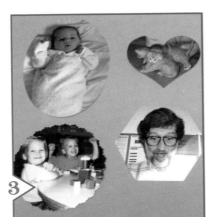

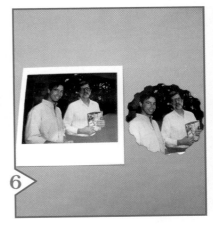

11

Tools

This section outlines some of the most essential tools of the craft and how to use them.

Stencils and templates come in literally hundreds of shapes and sizes, from simple circles and squares to very elaborate patterns. Although the terms "stencil" and "template" are often interchanged, there is a difference between them. Templates are used to trace shapes onto papers or photos with a pencil or pen, after which the shapes are cut out. Stencils are usually used as patterns to paint designs on a wall or furniture. However, when these same stencil patterns are traced onto paper, they can be colored with markers, used as die cuts or cut out to create elaborate mats or borders.

Scissors are available in many blade patterns and give the user many options for effects. They can be used in combination with traditional straight-edged scissors or other pattern-edged designs. Some hints to remember :

✂ Move the photo or paper you are cutting, rather than the scissors.

✂ For deep notches or angles, cut into the paper until you reach the point of the notch, then remove the scissors and cut toward the point from the other side. This is easier than trying to turn your scissors in a tight spot.

Tube wringers or paper corrugators (the center blue item and far left orange object) are wonderful to texture paper. They were originally sold as tools to press out every bit of paint from oil paint tubes.

Pattern-edged rulers are great tools for creating decorative borders and edges. They are sold separately, or sometimes come on the sides of templates.

The border for this section was created with Fiskars® Paper Edgers patterned scissors.

The designer chose to use straight-edged scissors here for an uncomplicated look. The interest comes from the layering of different papers. You could also place a different photo in each window pane.

(Santa pattern on page 140; banner pattern on page 83.)

Patterned Paper: Paper Patch®
Die Cut: Ellison® Craft & Design
Page Designer: Sharon Lewis for Memory Lane

A filmmaker's clapper board was the inspiration for this page, which is created by layering black and white papers. A white pen was used to add diagonal lines and "sprocket holes" to the black mats.

Patterned Paper: Paper Pizazz™ by Hot Off The Press
White Pen: ZIG® by EK Success Ltd.
Page Designer: Anne-Marie Spencer for Hot Off The Press

At Old Wardour Castle in England, we saw the filming of "Robin Hood, Prince of Thieves". We even got to pose with a prop sword!

"Bumping out" the photo—
that is, trimming it so the
subject extends beyond the
mat— adds dimension and
interest to a page.

Scissors: Fiskars® Paper
Edgers
Stickers: ©Mrs.
Grossman's
Paper Co.
Page Designer: Sharon
Lewis for
Memory Lane

Gone Fishin'

The worst day fishing
is better than
the best day working!

FISH ON!

IN THE NET...

WOW!

JOE CAUGHT THIS
27 LB. CHINOOK ON
A GUIDED FISHING
TRIP DOWN THE
CLACKAMAS RIVER.

Bumping out the fishing pole and the net
exaggerates the action and creates an
impression of movement.

Patterned Paper: Paper Pizazz™ by Hot Off
The Press
Scissors: Fiskars® Paper Edgers
Stickers: ©Mrs. Grossman's Paper Co.
Page Designer: Anne-Marie Spencer for
Hot Off The Press

The stripes on the flag were created by cutting red paper with a single pair of scissors, then flipping the paper to do the other side. This technique creates two opposite scissors patterns.

Patterned Paper: Paper Patch®
Scissors: Fiskars® Paper Edgers
Page Designer: LeNae Gerig for Hot Off The Press

Reversing the scissors pattern (by turning the scissors over) on each mat gives them different looks. Cut the first mat, reverse the scissors for the second, then reverse again for the third mat.

Patterned Paper: Paper Pizazz™ by Hot Off The Press
Scissors: Fiskars® Paper Edgers
Page Designer: LeNae Gerig for Hot Off The Press

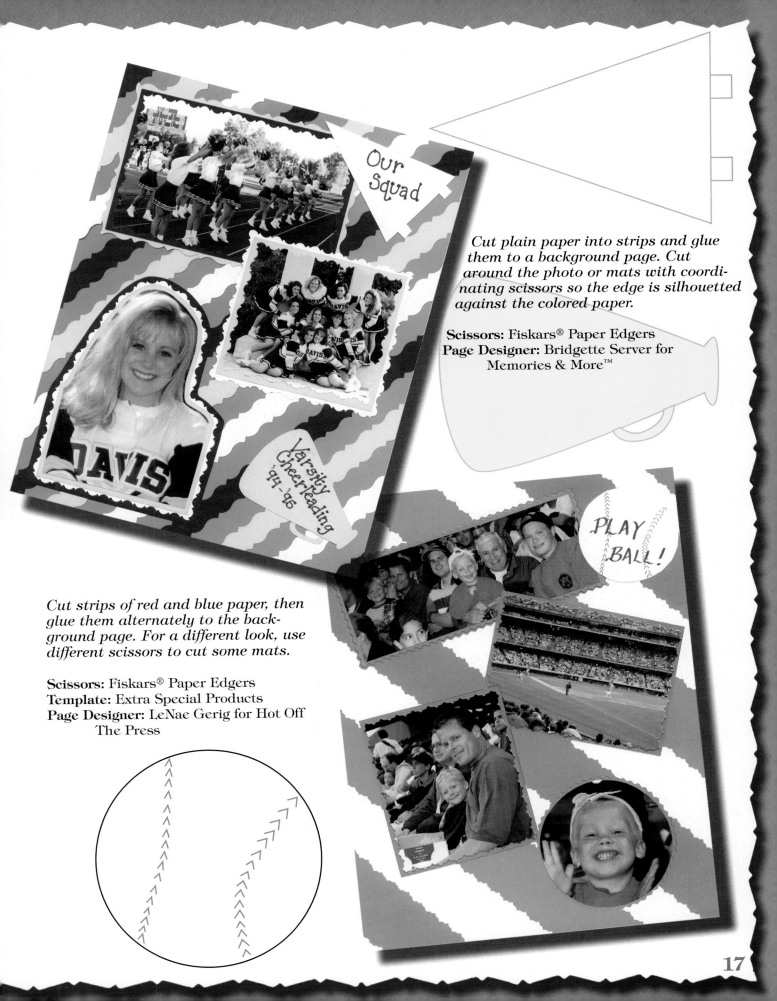

Our Squad

Cut plain paper into strips and glue them to a background page. Cut around the photo or mats with coordinating scissors so the edge is silhouetted against the colored paper.

Scissors: Fiskars® Paper Edgers
Page Designer: Bridgette Server for Memories & More™

DAVIS

Varsity Cheerleading '94-'95

PLAY BALL!

Cut strips of red and blue paper, then glue them alternately to the background page. For a different look, use different scissors to cut some mats.

Scissors: Fiskars® Paper Edgers
Template: Extra Special Products
Page Designer: LeNae Gerig for Hot Off The Press

Corner edgers can be used to create many interesting effects that regular decorative scissors cannot. For example, mat your photo on one color paper, then trim the corners so no mat shows. Mat on a contrasting paper, then trim those corners with the same edger.

Patterned Paper: Down Printing
Scissors: Fiskars® Corner Edgers
Computer Typeface: D.J. Inkers™
Stickers: Suzy's Zoo®
Page Designer: Brenda Cosgrove for Pebbles In My Pocket

To create decorative photo corners, use corner edgers to trim off paper corners, then glue the corner pieces to the corners of a photo. Mat the photo and place it on a page embellished with die cuts and patterned paper. A baseball pattern is on page 17.

Scissors: Fiskars® Corner Edgers
Die Cut: Ellison® Craft & Design
Patterned Paper: Paper Patch®
Page Designer: Brenda Birrell for Pebbles In My Pocket

ZACHARY TYLER
JONES

BORN MAY 1, 1996

7 LBS. 2 OZ.
20 1/2" LONG

Journal on white paper using a computer or typewriter. Use a template to draw an image around the journaling. Cut out the image, mat on colored paper and trim with decorative scissors.

Patterned Paper: Paper Patch®
Punch: Fiskars®
Scissors: Fiskars® Paper Edgers
Template: Provo Craft®
Page Designer: Anne-Marie Spencer for Hot Off The Press

Cut the top and bottom off a patterned sheet with decorative scissors and glue to a plain background sheet. For a finishing touch, use a template to cut some additional shapes, mat them and journal on the shapes.

Patterned Paper: Paper Pizazz™ by Hot Off The Press
Scissors: Fiskars® Paper Edgers
Template: Provo Craft®
Page Designer: Anne-Marie Spencer for Hot Off The Press

ANDREW AND BENJAMIN

SEEING DOUBLE

Use a circle cutter to cut out the wreath, then use straight scissors to indent "leaves" around the inner and outer edges. Use a template to cut out the photos, then trim the mats with decorative scissors. Embellish the page with bows and stickers (bow pattern on page 141).

Patterned Paper: Paper Pizazz™ by Hot Off The Press
Circle Cutter: Family Treasures
Stickers: ©Mrs. Grossman's Paper Co.
Scissors: Fiskars® Paper Edgers
Template: Déjà Views™ by C-Thru®
Page Designer: Anne-Marie Spencer for Hot Off The Press

Use templates to cut out the photos. Trim the photos and mats with varied straight and decorative scissors. Finish by cutting out elements from the cut-off sections of the photos to embellish the page.

Template: Déjà Views™ by C-Thru®
Scissors: Fiskars® Paper Edgers
Page Designer: Anne-Marie Spencer for Hot Off The Press

Trace a template onto a mat, then cut both inside and outside the template line to create a narrow outline which can be used as a mat over a photo or as a reverse template.

Patterned Paper: Paper Pizazz™ by Hot Off The Press
Template: Déjà Views™ by C-Thru®
Scissors: Fiskars® Paper Edgers
Page Designer: Anne-Marie Spencer for Hot Off the Press

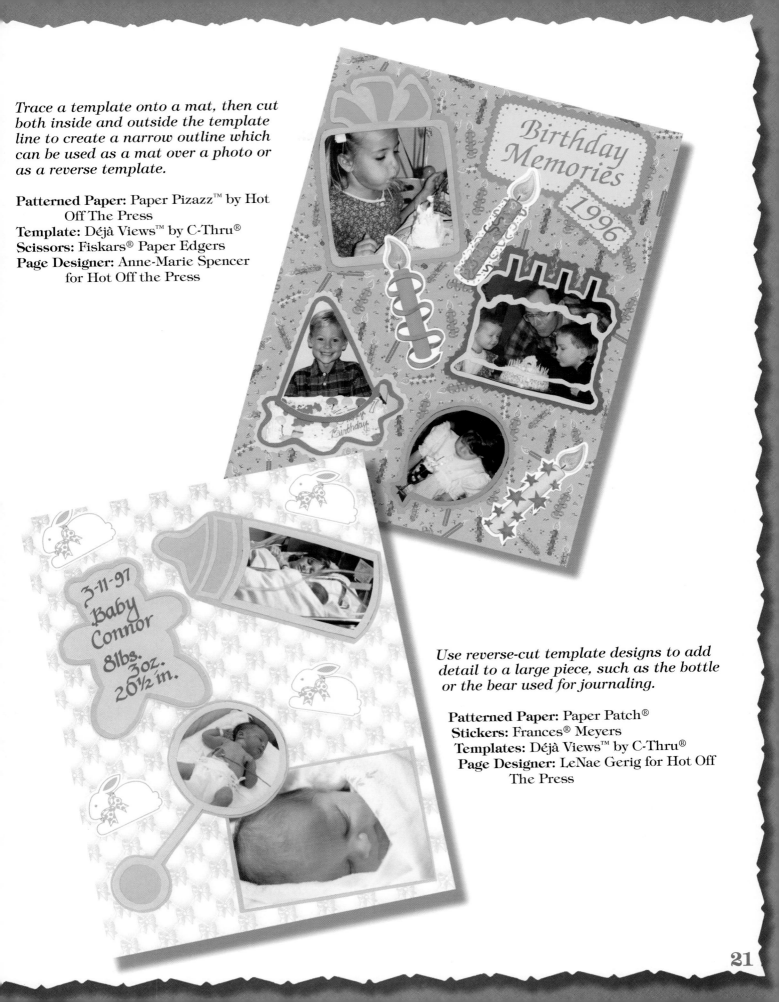

Use reverse-cut template designs to add detail to a large piece, such as the bottle or the bear used for journaling.

Patterned Paper: Paper Patch®
Stickers: Frances® Meyers
Templates: Déjà Views™ by C-Thru®
Page Designer: LeNae Gerig for Hot Off The Press

Instead of cutting out a stencil, color it in using acid-free pens. Stencil around the photo for a border.

Patterned Paper: Paper Pizazz™ by Hot Off The Press
Scissors: Fiskars® Paper Edgers
Stencil: StenSource International, Inc.
Page Designer: Anne-Marie Spencer for Hot Off The Press

MOMMY'S LITTLE ANGEL

Our new puppy
Bailey
6 weeks old

Color with a stencil similar to the pattern of the paper to make a border.

Patterned Paper: Paper Patch®
Stencil: StenSource International, Inc.
Scissors: Fiskars® Paper Edgers
Page Designer: LeNae Gerig for Hot Off The Press

22

Trace the stencil onto a solid sheet of paper and use a craft knife to cut it out. If there is a thin line that goes all the way around, leave small spaces to connect the parts. Use an oval template to cut around the stencil as shown, then use it to mat the photo. Notice the use of the decorative scissors on the photo, making the inner mat look ornate.

Patterned Paper: Paper Pizazz™ by Hot Off The Press
Scissors: Fiskars® Paper Edgers
Craft Knife: X-acto®
Stencil: StenSource International, Inc.
Page Designer: Anne-Marie Spencer for Hot Off The Press

Carefully tracing and cutting out stencils to mat photos gives your page a Victorian look that works well with formal or black and white photos. The stencil looks beautiful when used on the journaling papers, too.

Craft Knife: X-acto®
Stencil: StenSource International, Inc.
Velour Paper: Hygloss Product, Inc.
Page Designer: Anne-Marie Spencer for Hot Off The Press

Janette Elizabeth
Parents-Don and Sylvia
Born Nov 8, 1965

Anne-Marie Victoria
Parents-Don and Sylvia
Born March 27, 1962

Use two pattern rulers and different paper colors to create "water" for a wave effect at the bottom of the page. Continue the beach theme with an umbrella and beach stickers.

Patterned Paper: Paper Pizazz™ by Hot Off The Press
Scissors: Fiskars® Paper Edgers
Stickers: ©Mrs. Grossman's Paper Co.
Rulers: Déjà Views™ by C-Thru®
Template: Déjà Views™ by C-Thru®
Page Designer: Anne-Marie Spencer for Hot Off The Press

Create a spectacular border by using a pattern ruler to make a border for a page, then trace and cut a separate stencil on one edge.

Patterned Paper: Paper Patch®
Scissors: Fiskars® Paper Edgers
Stencil: StenSource International, Inc.
Ruler: Déjà Views™ by C-Thru®
Template: Déjà Views™ by C-Thru®
Page Designer: Anne-Marie Spencer for Hot Off The Press

If you can't find a stencil or template to match the theme of your photos, draw your own design and use it to cut the mat and photos into shapes (the sailboat pattern is on page 141). Mat and trim with decorative scissors.

Patterned Paper: Paper Pizazz™ by Hot Off The Press
Scissors: Fiskars® Paper Edgers
Template: Déjà Views™ by C-Thru®
Page Designer: Anne-Marie Spencer for Hot Off The Press

Add a few details to a simple shape like a circle, and you will be amazed at what you can create. Decorative scissors can disguise many flaws, so don't be afraid of making your own designs.

Patterned Paper: Paper Pizazz™ by Hot Off The Press
Scissors: Fiskars® Paper Edgers
Page Designer: Anne-Marie Spencer for Hot Off The Press

Papers

Paper is the absolute essential for making memory albums. Since becoming aware of the need for acid-free and lignin-free papers, manufacturers have produced many different patterns relating to a vast array of occasions. Papers are available by the sheet, in packages or in books by theme. Also, acid-free and lignin-free foil papers, neon papers, paper doilies and metallic embossed papers are available for memory albums.

Almost all the paper on the market is sized at a standard 8½"x11". Since albums come in many sizes and there are differences in foreign paper standards, creativity and imagination can help adapt the paper to use; after all, this activity is based on cutting and embellishing! Borders of different colors and patterns can be added to the tops or sides to elongate a background sheet, or the paper can be cut in sections and arranged on a larger album page. As with many tools in making memory albums, you have lots of options.

Patterned papers are available in generic dots, checks, stripes and such. Themed papers provide a great look with little time investment. For instance, a paper of water drops can be used with photos of a pool party, beach visit, playing in the sprinkler, walking in the rain or white-water rafting. A sheet of cookies goes with photos of cookie making, cookie eating, cookie giving or Girl Scouts selling cookies—wow!

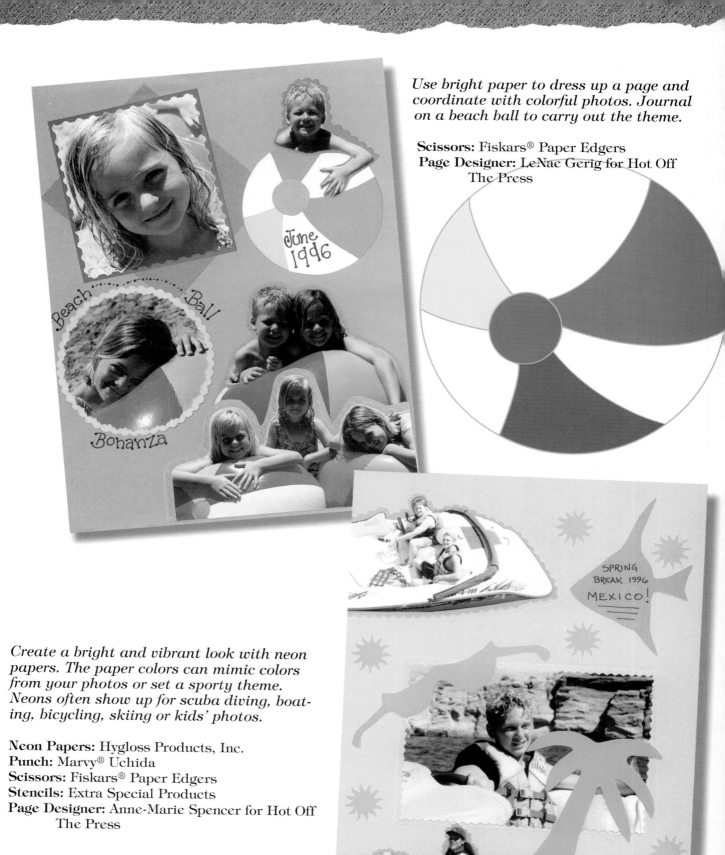

Use bright paper to dress up a page and coordinate with colorful photos. Journal on a beach ball to carry out the theme.

Scissors: Fiskars® Paper Edgers
Page Designer: LeNae Gerig for Hot Off The Press

June 1996

Beach Ball
Bonanza

SPRING BREAK 1996 MEXICO!

Create a bright and vibrant look with neon papers. The paper colors can mimic colors from your photos or set a sporty theme. Neons often show up for scuba diving, boating, bicycling, skiing or kids' photos.

Neon Papers: Hygloss Products, Inc.
Punch: Marvy® Uchida
Scissors: Fiskars® Paper Edgers
Stencils: Extra Special Products
Page Designer: Anne-Marie Spencer for Hot Off The Press

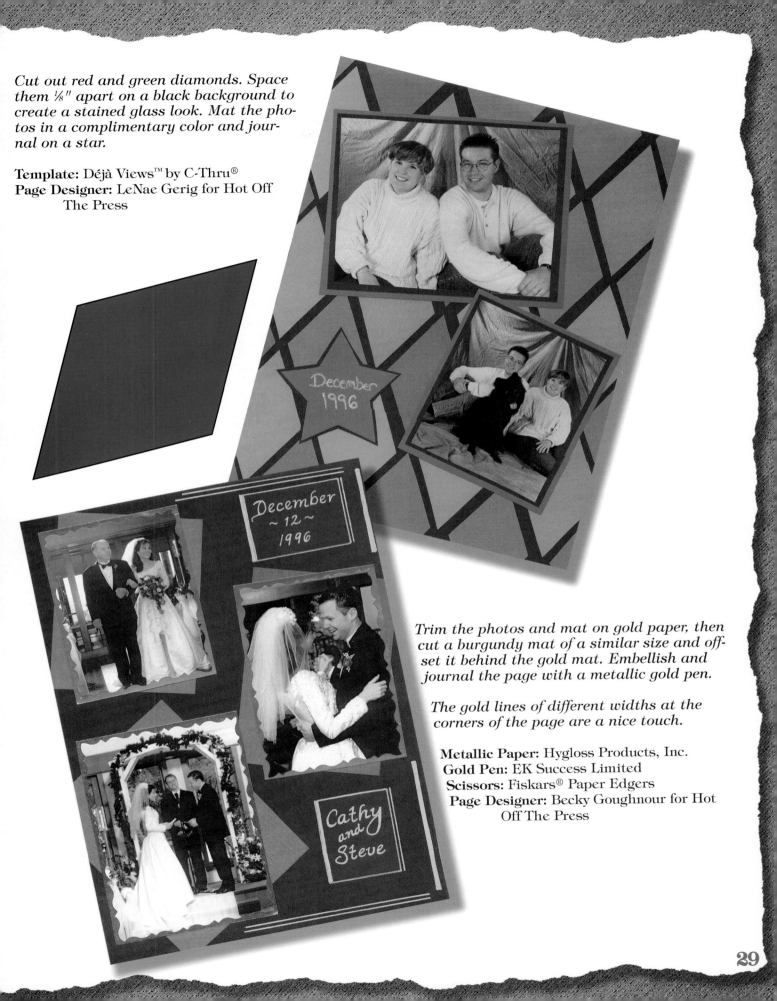

Cut out red and green diamonds. Space them ⅛" apart on a black background to create a stained glass look. Mat the photos in a complimentary color and journal on a star.

Template: Déjà Views™ by C-Thru®
Page Designer: LeNae Gerig for Hot Off The Press

December 1996

December
~ 12 ~
1996

Cathy and Steve

Trim the photos and mat on gold paper, then cut a burgundy mat of a similar size and offset it behind the gold mat. Embellish and journal the page with a metallic gold pen.

The gold lines of different widths at the corners of the page are a nice touch.

Metallic Paper: Hygloss Products, Inc.
Gold Pen: EK Success Limited
Scissors: Fiskars® Paper Edgers
Page Designer: Becky Goughnour for Hot Off The Press

Pick a plain color for the background, then cut another color into strips with decorative scissors. Place these strips evenly spaced across the background sheet.

Make a 4"x6½"postcard using plain paper and a photo. The journaling on the side can tell about the photos. Don't forget to add a "postmark" with the date!

Scissors: Fiskars® Paper Edgers
Sun Stencil: StenSource International, Inc.
Page Designer: Anne-Marie Spencer for Hot Off The Press

Hi, everybody!
I'm at Disneyworld with mom, dad and Grandma. I got to ride on the prettiest horse on the carousel and then we spun around in this really big teacup. I'm having lots of fun, wish you were here.
Love,
Madison

MARK Joins ~ The Marines GRADUATING from BOOT CAMP

JANUARY 1996

PUTTING ON CAMMIES

WITH LITTLE BROTHER JEFF

Mat photos on plain paper and use a patterned background sheet that relates to the photos. Closely crop a photo to make a silhouette, mat it on light paper and journal on the mat around the photo.

Patterned Paper: Paper Pizazz™ by Hot Off The Press
Punch: McGill, Inc.
Stencils: Déjà Views™ by C-Thru®
Page Designer: Becky Goughnour for Hot Off The Press

Use theme stickers like these cherries to create a unified look on a page. Cut and mat your photos in similar shapes. An attractive way to present photos is to crop and mat them with a single sheet of colored paper. A circle cutter can be used to make perfectly round mats and photos to represent cherries. Simple shapes, such as the stems and leaves, can add a lot of interest to your page.

Circle Cutter: Family Treasures
Patterned Papers: Paper Patch®
Stickers: Mary Englebreit® for Melissa Neufeld, Inc.
Page Designer: Sharon Lewis for Memory Lane

The look of total.... concentration.

Nov. 1996

Juliette's Sweet Taste of Success!

To increase the color and depth of a photo, mat it on two contrasting colors. Mount the matted photos on a background sheet that celebrates the occasion. The wavy music staff was drawn directly on the background paper.

Die Cuts: Ellison® Craft & Design
Patterned Paper: Paper Pizazz™ by Hot Off The Press
Page Designer: Joy Hulsh for Pebbles In My Pocket

™ & ©Ellison® Craft & Design

HAPPY BIRTHDAY TO YOU

Abby turns 2

Matting with solid and patterned papers can increase interest as well as adding color and depth to the page. Overlapping the photos allows more to be placed on the page.

Patterned Papers: Paper Patch®
Stickers: Frances Meyer Inc.®
Scissors: Fiskars® Paper Edgers
Page Designer: LeNae Gerig for Hot Off The Press

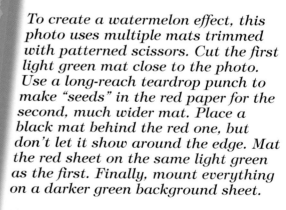

To create a watermelon effect, this photo uses multiple mats trimmed with patterned scissors. Cut the first light green mat close to the photo. Use a long-reach teardrop punch to make "seeds" in the red paper for the second, much wider mat. Place a black mat behind the red one, but don't let it show around the edge. Mat the red sheet on the same light green as the first. Finally, mount everything on a darker green background sheet.

Punch: McGill, Inc.
Scissors: Family Treasures
Page Designer: Channa Brewer for Memory Lane

Edge the plaid paper and glue on
the background page at an angle.
Trim the edges which fall outside
the background page. Double-mat
the photos with a plain color and a
silver paper positioned at an angle
behind the photos.

Metallic Paper: Hygloss Products, Inc.
Patterned Paper: Paper Pizazz™ by Hot
Off The Press
Scissors: Fiskars® Paper Edgers
Page Designer: LeNae Gerig for Hot Off
The Press

For a country theme, make stitches
and dots around the single mats.
Place a brown mat behind it off center. Complete the look with a pumpkin
die cut to journal on.

Patterned Paper: Paper Patch®
Die Cut: Family Treasures™
Scissors: Fiskars® Paper Edgers
Page Designer: LeNae Gerig for Hot Off
The Press

To carry a theme throughout a page, cut apart excess photos and use the images as mats around larger photos. For example, the exercise balls and weights were lined up in rows. These photos were trimmed, matted and placed over other photos as borders or mats.

Patterned Papers: Paper Pizazz™ by Hot Off The Press
Page Designer: Anne-Marie Spencer for Hot Off The Press

Whole photos of Stonehenge were enlarged on a color copier, cut apart and used to mat the original photos.

Page Designer: Anne-Marie Spencer for Hot Off The Press

For a polished look, use two paper patterns that coordinate. Rather than laying the patterns against one other, use a plain paper to accent them. Here each photo is double-matted on first a patterned, then a plain sheet, then mounted on the patterned background paper.

The large chalkboard was made from plain paper and the small boards were cut from another sheet of patterned paper. The house pattern is on page 141.

Patterned Papers: Paper Patch®
Page Designer: Anne-Marie Spencer
for Hot Off The Press

These snowy photos are matted with white paper trimmed. This looks good with the snow theme. Use plain white paper to separate the patterned mat from the same background paper. The trees and star are cut with various sizes of stencils.

Patterned Papers: Paper Patch®
Starburst Template: Déjà Views™
Trees Template: Provo Craft®
Scissors: Fiskars® Paper Edgers
Page Designer: Becky Goughnour
for Hot Off The Press

35

Use plain brown paper to mat the photos and yellow paper to make the sunflower petals. The mat matches the girls' dresses, which match the background paper, providing a charming repetition.

Also notice the many layers of mats used on this page. The black-and-white dotted background is double-matted with a yellow-and-white checked pattern and the sunflower sheet.

Patterned Papers: Paper Patch®
Scissors: Fiskars® Paper Edgers
Page Designer: LeNae Gerig for Hot Off The Press

petal

Instead of cropping photos in plain ovals, cut them in shapes to coordinate with the background paper—like this football (pattern on page 141).

Patterned Papers: Paper Pizazz™ by Hot Off The Press
Scissors: Fiskars® Paper Edgers
Page Designer: LeNae Gerig for Hot Off The Press

Mix different types of papers such as plain, glossy and this doily used as a curtain. Ruler templates were used for the valence and fence. Two colors of brown paper were used for the flower pots. Cut identical pots from each color and cut away the right side of the dark one. Take square snips out of the cut side to resemble an uneven shadow. Glue to the left side of the light pot.

Patterned Paper: Paper Pizazz™ by Hot Off The Press
Doilies: Hygloss Products, Inc.
Scissors: Fiskars® Paper Edgers
Flowers Template: Provo Craft®
Page Designer: Anne-Marie Spencer for Hot Off The Press

Mixing textures gives added interest to pages. For example, combining black velour paper and silver paper doilies creates an elegant look with black and white photos.

Velour, Metallic, and Shiny Papers: Hygloss Products, Inc.
Doilies: Hygloss Products, Inc.
Punch: Marvy® Uchida
Page Designer: Anne-Marie Spencer for Hot Off The Press

Dorothy Price and William White

August 9, 1947

To create a woven background, cut vertical strips every ½" in a plain colored paper. Cut two different patterned papers into ½" strips. Glue one end of one to the back of the page and weave between vertical strips. Glue one end of the other to the front of the paper and weave the opposite way. Repeat to the bottom of the page.

This photo is double-matted with a plaid paper and a light plain paper in colors which repeat those of the woven background. The brown cattails are a final detail taken from the background of the photo itself.

Patterned Papers: MPR Paperbilities™
Scissors: Fiskars® Paper Edgers
Page Designer: Anne-Marie Spencer for Hot Off The Press

Use the above method with ¼" strips to create these woven eggs. With decorative scissors, cut frames to glue over the eggs. Mat the photos on paper covered with punches, then trim with patterned scissors. Add a few punches to the background sheet. Be sure to cut your photos in different sizes for variety. Don't be afraid to cut one photo in a silhouette, even if all the others are ovals.

Punches: McGill, Inc.
Scissors: Fiskars® Paper Edgers
Page Designer: Anne-Marie Spencer for Hot Off The Press

This quilt page is simpler than it appears with the use of a cube ruler template. Trace three to five cubes onto five different papers. Cut out the cubes, then cut each into three diamonds. Rearrange the pieces into many cubes, each with different-patterned sides. Notice on this page that the same three patterns always form the cube and two different patterns divide the cubes. Alternate patterned cubes with photos as shown. Trim the background paper and glue to a larger sheet, then journal.

Patterned Papers: MPR Paperbilities™
Ruler Template: Family Treasures
Page Designer: Anne-Marie Spencer for Hot Off The Press

A simpler method of making a quilt is to cut squares of patterned paper (these are 2½" square) and cut your photos to the same size. Glue them to a larger sheet of paper, alternating photos and papers.

Patterned Papers: MPR Paperbilities™
Scissors: Fiskars® Paper Edgers
Page Designer: Anne-Marie Spencer for Hot Off The Press

Make packages by matting photos with brightly colored paper, then cut ¼" strips of paper in contrasting colors. Glue the strips directly over the photos, placing them so the action is not obscured. Cut thinner strips for the ribbon centers. Cut a bow and glue to the "package" top. Embellish the page with party stickers.

Patterned Papers: Paper Pizazz™ by Hot Off The Press
Scissors: Fiskars® Paper Edgers
Stickers: Frances Meyer Inc.®
Page Designer: LeNae Gerig for Hot Off The Press

Another means of giving photos a gift-wrap look is to cut rectangles from patterned papers to represent a box and lid. Mat with plain paper and cut strips of a contrasting color for ribbons. Trim the photo into an oval or circle and place it over the large rectangle as if emerging from the box. Glue the lid above the photo at an angle as if hinged. Top off the gift with a bow sticker and a tag to journal on.

Patterned Papers: Paper Pizazz™ by Hot Off The Press
Scissors: Fiskars® Paper Edgers
Stickers: ©Mrs. Grossman's Paper Co.
Page Designer: LeNae Gerig for Hot Off The Press

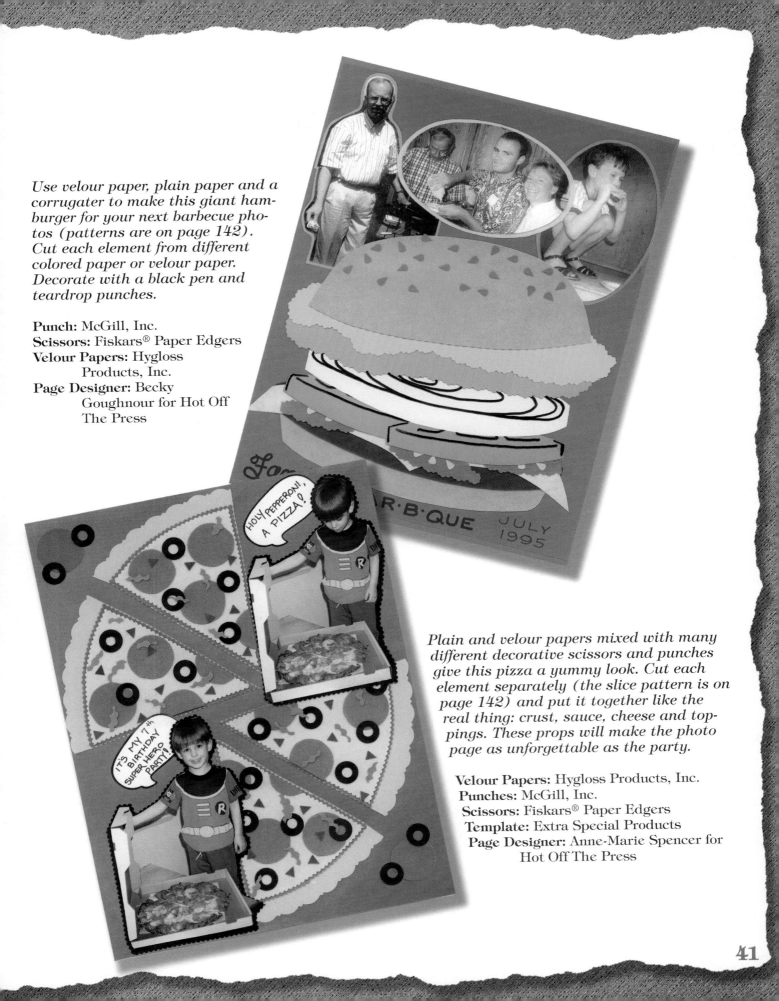

Use velour paper, plain paper and a corrugater to make this giant hamburger for your next barbecue photos (patterns are on page 142). Cut each element from different colored paper or velour paper. Decorate with a black pen and teardrop punches.

Punch: McGill, Inc.
Scissors: Fiskars® Paper Edgers
Velour Papers: Hygloss Products, Inc.
Page Designer: Becky Goughnour for Hot Off The Press

Plain and velour papers mixed with many different decorative scissors and punches give this pizza a yummy look. Cut each element separately (the slice pattern is on page 142) and put it together like the real thing: crust, sauce, cheese and toppings. These props will make the photo page as unforgettable as the party.

Velour Papers: Hygloss Products, Inc.
Punches: McGill, Inc.
Scissors: Fiskars® Paper Edgers
Template: Extra Special Products
Page Designer: Anne-Marie Spencer for Hot Off The Press

41

DANIEL

Rhonda
Summer of 1996

Stationery

When memory albums exploded onto the national scene, scrapbookers were clamoring for product, often before many retailers were aware of the activity and what products they needed to carry to support it. Acid-free stationery offered a solution to the problem, as it was already nationally distributed and easily accessible to the retail consumer.

Stationery is usually available in 8½"x11" or 5½"x8½" sheets with designs only along the border. It is easy to work with and can be utilized in a number of ways. If you are looking for a quick and easy border or frame for portraits, the wide variety of imprintables (as some stationery is known in the trade) are a great solution. While this is the most common use for stationery, we've gathered some more creative ways to use this form of decorative papers.

The border for this section was created using a corner punch from Family Treasures.

Cut elements from a piece of stationery (like these rattles and hearts) and use them to embellish a patterned background sheet. Notice that all four corners have the same design, creating a framed effect.

Patterned Paper: Paper Patch®
Scissors: Fiskars® Paper Edgers
Stationery: Frances® Meyer, Inc.
Page Designer: LeNae Gerig for Hot Off The Press

The designer cut the watermelons from a small sheet of stationery and placed them in two corners. The other two corners were filled with red triangles. The watermelon theme is continued by cutting the photos into watermelon shapes and double-matting them in red and green.

Patterned Paper: Paper Patch®
Stationery: Frances® Meyer, Inc.
Scissors: Fiskars® Paper Edgers
Page Designer: LeNae Gerig for Hot Off The Press

44

By using two sizes of coordinating stationery, you can create an easy border around a photo and the entire page. Be sure to add some plain colored mats to emphasize the border colors.

Stationery: Frances® Meyer, Inc.
Scissors: Family Treasures
Page Designer: LeNae Gerig for Hot Off The Press

Rhonda
Summer of 1996

A quick and easy method of creating a page is to simply mat a photo on a sheet of stationery and use coordinating background sheets for the rest of the page.

Stationery: Frances® Meyer, Inc.
Scissors: Fiskars® Paper Edgers
Page Designer: LeNae Gerig for Hot Off The Press

This elaborate page is easier than you think. Mat the picture with different sizes of stationery and plain paper, then embellish the outside of the page with gimp trim. Finally, cut pansies from some stationery and glue one onto each corner.

Stationery: Sonburn
Gimp: William E. Wright Ltd.
Scissors: Fiskars® Paper Edgers
Page Designer: Anne-Marie Spencer for Hot Off The Press

With stationery, there is often a large blank space in the middle of the page. One way to draw the pictures and border together is by using stickers or coordinating mats. This page creatively uses pencil and crayon stickers to make a second border which moves toward the photos in the middle of the page.

Stationery: Sonburn
Scissors: Fiskars® Paper Edgers
Stickers: ©Mrs. Grossman's Paper Co.
Page Designer: LeNae Gerig for Hot Off The Press

South Padre Island

Summer Fun

We had a wonderful vacation on the beach!

Summer 1996

Offset the matted photo inside the blank center space. Use templates to cut the fish and suns to embellish and journal on.

Stationery: Sonburn
Template: Déjà Views by C-Thru®
Page Designer: Janye Anderson for Sonburn

Punch the corners of the stationery with a corner punch. Journal on a coordinating die cut. Notice how one die cut has been placed behind another as a shadow.

Die Cut: Ellison® Craft & Design
Punch: Family Treasures
Stationery: Sonburn
Page Designer: Janye Anderson for Sonburn

Baby Ballerina

™ & ©Ellison® Craft & Design

47

If you have two pieces of stationery with similar themes—such as a large sheet and a note card—mount a photo on the smaller piece. Embellish the page with tulips or other flowers cut from plain paper.

Stationery: Gussie's
Page Designer: Gina Barker for Gussie's

Cut the apples and watermelons from plain paper. Apples falling from the tree and resting on the photos tie in with the background stationery.

Stationery: Gussie's
Page Designer: Gina Barker for Gussie's

Cut the gloves, shovels, watering can and wheelbarrow from another note card and place around the photos matted on flowered stationery.

Stationery: Gussie's
Page Designer: Gina Barker
    for Gussie's

Embellish themed stationery by cutting fish or other small objects from a note card. Place these cutouts around the matted photos. Take a sequence of photos to show action such as a boy jumping into a pool.

Stationery: Gussie's
Page Designer: Gina Barker for Gussie's

49

Stickers

Stickers provide an easy way to add graphic design elements to a page. It's very easy to get lost in the wide array of stickers that are available. In the past, stickers have been designed for children, who have long collected and traded them. Today, manufacturers realize the need for memory albums and have expanded their selections to include themed stickers for virtually every occasion. There are stickers that relate to jobs and hobbies. There are sticker letters and numbers to use in journaling. There are beautiful and elaborate stickers to echo the elegance of the Victorian era. There are cute stickers, botanical stickers, sticker borders—and the list continues to grow!

Stickers are quite easy to work with (just peel and stick), although you should be sure of placement before application because, once applied, they are difficult to remove without tearing your paper. Stickers can be used to create a background, to tie in with the action or theme of photos, or to create a border on a page. They can add that "finishing touch" to a page or fill in blank areas. They can be layered to create bouquets or gardens and can be used on either papers or photos. Be sure any stickers that are applied to photos are acid-free in both the paper and adhesive.

The border for this section was created using a ruler template from Déjà Views by C-Thru®.

There are so many beautiful stickers available that it is easy to coordinate stickers with stationery, patterned paper or borders. This page expertly uses stickers that match the stationery around the photos.

Stationery: Mara Mi
Stickers: The Gifted Line®
Page Designer: Allison Myers for Memory Lane

Use stickers that reflect the feel of the papers to bring your photos and the area around them together. Notice how the monkeys hang or stand on the photos, and how the zebra appears to enter the photo from the greenery at the side.

Stationery: Sonburn
Scissors: Fiskars® Paper Edgers
Stickers: ©Mrs. Grossman's Paper Co.
Page Designer: LeNae Gerig for Hot Off The Press

our lil' **Chickadee**

Natalie's 1st Easter 1996

Another way to use stickers is to build the page around a sticker similar to an object in the photo. The chick stickers on this page reflect the stuffed toy in the baby's hands.

Patterned Paper: Paper Patch®
Stickers: Suzy's Zoo®
Page Designer: Allison Myers for Memory Lane

Stickers are a fast and easy way of strengthening the theme of a page. These golf stickers are a perfect embellishment for this page. Notice the tiny golf balls that add a finished look to otherwise empty spaces.

Stickers: ©Mrs. Grossman's Paper Co.
Scissors: Fiskars® Paper Edgers
Page Designer: Bridgette Server for Memories & More™

Have some of the stickers actually overlap your photos. It really brings the stickers to life and it can even help hold down your photos or hide a mistake in cutting. Notice the clever way journaling is done around the photos and stickers.

Stickers: Provo Craft®
Patterned Paper: Paper Pizazz™ by Hot Off
    The Press
Scissors: Fiskars® Paper Edgers
Page Designer: Anne-Marie Spencer for Hot
    Off The Press

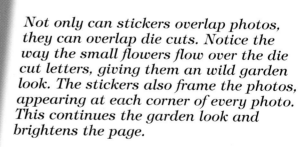

Not only can stickers overlap photos, they can overlap die cuts. Notice the way the small flowers flow over the die cut letters, giving them an wild garden look. The stickers also frame the photos, appearing at each corner of every photo. This continues the garden look and brightens the page.

Die Cuts: Ellison® Craft & Design
Stickers: ©Mrs. Grossman's Paper Co.
Page Designer: Channa Brewer for
    Memory Lane

The "patterned" paper in the background is actually a plain white sheet covered in stickers. The illusion of a patterned page is created by making some of the stickers seem to flow off the page or hide behind the mats. Carefully matting the photos in many different colors helps keep the background page from getting monotonous.

Patterned Paper: Paper Patch®
Stickers: ©Mrs. Grossman's Paper Co.
Page Designer: Channa Brewer for Memory Lane

The blocks from the photos suggest the theme for this brightly colored page. Crop your photos into block-like shapes, then put brightly colored stickers in similar shapes around them for a border.

Stickers: ©Mrs. Grossman's Paper Co.
Page Designer: LeNae Gerig for Hot Off
      The Press

Create your own borders on a patterned paper with stickers that suit the theme of the page. Tilt a few stickers so the border doesn't look too rigid.

Patterned Paper: Paper Pizazz™ by Hot Off The Press
Scissors: Fiskars® Paper Edgers
Stickers: ©Mrs. Grossman's Paper Co.
Template: Déjà Views™ by C-Thru®
Page Designer: Anne-Marie Spencer for Hot Off The Press

Put stickers all around the outside of a background page for a border, then add a smaller sheet in a contrasting color to give the appearance of having a patterned page underneath.

Patterned Paper: Paper Patch®
Die Cuts: Ellison® Craft & Design
Stickers: Stickopotamus™
Page Designer: Anne Smith for Memory Lane

™ & ©Ellison® Craft & Design

™ & ©Ellison® Craft & Design

The "vine" borders at the top and bottom of the page are created with overlapping rows and clusters of individual leaf stickers. This page is also an excellent example of how to use leftover scraps of patterned papers—cut them into 1½" squares to create a "quilt" look.

Patterned Papers: Paper Patch®
Stickers: ©Mrs. Grossman's Paper Co.
Rubber Stamps: D.O.T.S. Letter Stamps
Photo Corners: Boston International
Page Designer: Channa Brewer for Memory Lane

HEY, SIS - COVER YOUR EYES (SO I CAN EAT YOUR CARROTS)

OH SORRY, WAS THIS YOUR NACHO CHIP?

Kyle LOVES to eat! At our outdoor barbecue, he had a big lunch, followed by a popsicle (and a set of fresh clothes) then walked around and found more food on everyone's unattended plates!

HEY THIS TASTES BETTER THAN MY LEMONADE!

HAVENT YOU EVER GOTTEN MESSY?

WHAT ARE YOU LOOKING AT?

When using stickers to make a border, don't forget to consider where your photos will go. Have a few cover the border area. This can really help if there aren't enough stickers to go around the entire page. It also helps keep your page different and interesting. Look at the journaling on this page!

Stickers: Stickopotamus™
Scissors: Fiskars® Paper Edgers
White Pen: ZIG® by EK Success Ltd.
Page Designer: Anne-Marie Spencer for Hot Off The Press

Stickers can be just as important to a page as the photos, and, as with photos, don't be afraid to have a few overlap. Have the cat stand in front of the pumpkin or the ghost float over the cobweb. Also, put some stickers in and around your photos.

Scissors: Fiskars® Paper Edgers
Stickers: ©Mrs. Grossman's Paper Co.
Page Designer: Bridgette Server for Memories & More™

The paper roads are a great beginning, but the stickers add so much to this page. The fire truck emphasizes Bobby's fascination with his toys, and the hose and ladders help bring the different areas of the page together.

Scissors: Fiskars® Paper Edgers
Stickers: ©Mrs. Grossman's Paper Co.
Page Designer: Anne-Marie Spencer for Hot Off The Press

Rectangular stickers with country themes make a great patchwork quilt to frame a photo. Arrange as shown to create an easy quilt look for any page.

Patterned Paper: Paper Patch®
Stickers: Provo Craft®
Page Designer: Anne-Marie Spencer for Hot Off The Press

If you have many small pictures, try making a quilt with stickers and pictures. The trick is to cut paper squares the same size as your pictures and alternate them. Cut thin strips of paper the same color as the background and put them over the seams between the pictures and patches. Finally, place stickers on the paper squares as shown.

White Pen: ZIG® by EK Success Ltd.
Stickers: Provo Craft®
Page Designer: Anne-Marie Spencer for Hot Off The Press

Birthday Kaitlin!

7 years old

Instead of a party this year, Kate asked for a new ten speed bike. Dad, Mom, Grandpa Ren & Grandma Connie all pitched in and bought Kaitlin a new hot pink ten spee... She loved it! Haley Morris, Genevieve ... Uncle Steve, Aunt Deanna, Sierra and J... all came to have pizza and cake and ice cr... and wish Kaitlin a very Happy Birthday...

FISKARS

Family Treasures

Family Treasures

MARVY

41

May 1996

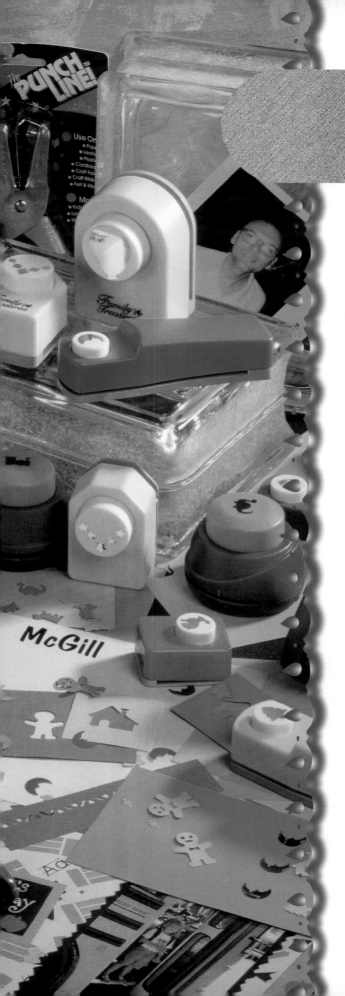

Punches

Given the variety of punches available and the many ways to use them, it's conceivable that a book could be written on this topic alone. Available as borders, corner treatments, shapes and figures, punches can be used in a variety of ways. Used on background sheets, mats and photographs, they punch out images through which the paper underneath will then show. The punched-out sections can be used like stickers or die cuts.

Like many tools used in memory albums, punches are quickly evolving. They now come in elaborate shapes, with long handles (to reach farther into papers), as intricate corner cutters and with a row of designs on one punch. The following pages offer lots of ways to use some of the hundreds of punches available.

The border for this section was created using Fiskars® Paper Edgers and McGill punches.

After the photos are matted and the journaling is done, the page may still need a few extra touches. Punches provide an easy way to embellish a page. Just punch out many different shapes from brightly colored paper and scatter them around the page. Add a few strips of paper cut with decorative scissors to vary the sizes of the objects.

Punches: Fiskars®
Scissors: Fiskars® Paper Edgers
Page Designer: Bridgette Server for Memories & More™

I am the dude, da baby rapper I like to dance around.

I wear my hat that's where it's at and make da funny sounds

L.L. Cool Dalton

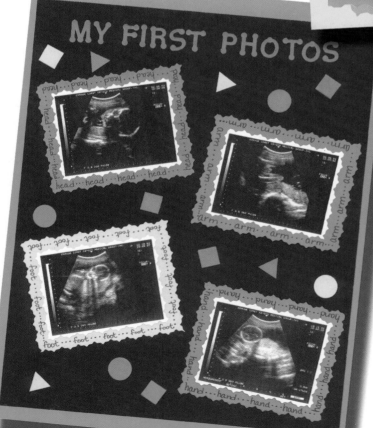

MY FIRST PHOTOS

Brightly colored punches look great evenly spaced against a black background. They pick up on the colors of the mats and make up for the lack of color in the photos themselves. Notice the clever journaling on the mats.

Punches: Fiskars®
Stickers: Memory Makers
Page Designer: Bridgette Server for Memories & More™

Use rows of punches to frame a page or make a border. Notice the double trees around the outside of the page, arranged as if one was the shadow of another. Great die-cut journaling and the dots and lines drawn around the page effectively bring all the elements together.

Die Cuts: Ellison® Craft & Design
Patterned Paper: Paper Patch®
Punch: Marvy® Uchida
Stationery: Mara Mi
Page Designer: Sonia Paulsen for Memory Lane

Cleverly coordinate punches and die cuts when possible—you will be surprised at how many similar items are available. In addition, punches are used to give the corner triangles extra panâche. The bike pattern is on page 140.

Die Cuts: Ellison® Craft & Design
Punches: Family Treasures
Page Designer: Becky Goughnour for Hot Off The Press

63

Embellish the page with punched balloons that match the mats. Use the balloons as a border on two sides, then complete the look with a festive "Happy Birthday" sticker.

Patterned Paper: Paper Pizazz™ by Hot Off The Press
Punch: Family Treasures
Stickers: Frances Meyer Inc.®
Page Designer: LeNae Gerig for Hot Off The Press

Punched umbrellas around the border echo the color of the patterned paper and the umbrellas cut from templates. Matting the photos in the same two colors gives this page a well-planned look.

Patterned Paper: Paper Pizazz™ by Hot Off The Press
Punch: Marvy® Uchida
Template: Extra Special Products
Page Designer: LeNae Gerig for Hot Off The Press

A photo taken in the woods is turned into an elegant theme page by matting it on forest-patterned paper. Punched leaves in two different shapes and colors are used to accent the wide border.

Patterned Paper: Paper Pizazz™ by Hot Off The Press
Punches: Family Treasures
Page Designer: LeNae Gerig for Hot Off The Press

Use punches that tie in with the theme of a page. These apple punches are the perfect complement to this school page. Two sizes of red apples give added depth and detail to the border. Notice the small apple punch is added to the 2¼"x1⅝" journaling chalkboard.

Patterned Paper: Paper Patch®
Punches: Marvy® Uchida
Page Designer: LeNae Gerig for Hot Off The Press

65

Create a theme by putting punches on the mats and border strips to accent the journaling. Notice that the cats are tilted and turned in different directions to vary their appearance.

Patterned Papers: Paper Pizazz™ by Hot Off The Press
Punch: Marvy® Uchida
Scissors: Fiskars® Paper Edgers
Page Designer: LeNae Gerig for Hot Off The Press

Arrange punches on paper strips across the top and bottom of the page to create a border. Alternate patterned and plain paper punches. Place a heart punch at each corner of the photo to bring the papers into the photos.

Patterned Paper: Paper Patch®
Punch: Marvy® Uchida
Scissors: Fiskars® Paper Edgers
Page Designer: LeNae Gerig for Hot Off The Press

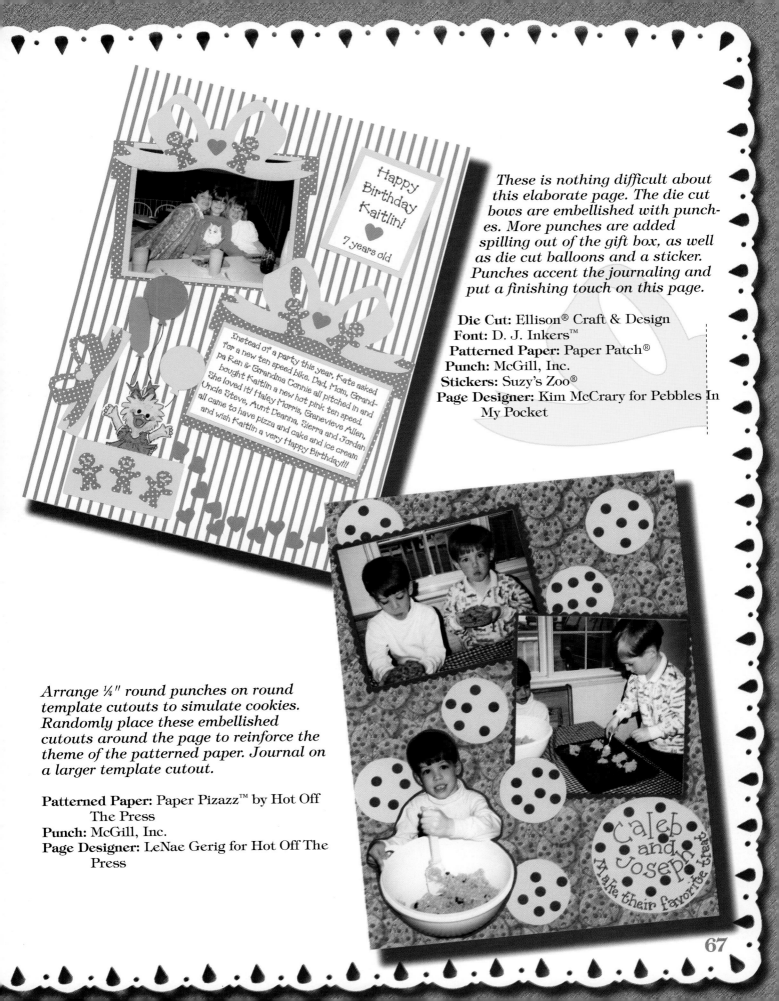

Happy
Birthday
Kaitlin!

♥

7 years old

Instead of a party this year, Kate asked
for a new ten speed bike. Dad, Mom, Grandpa Ren & Grandma Connie all pitched in and
bought Kaitlin a new hot pink ten speed.
She loved it! Haley Morris, Genevieve Allen,
Uncle Steve, Aunt Deanna, Sierra and Jordan
all came to have pizza and cake and ice cream
and wish Kaitlin a very Happy Birthday!!!

These is nothing difficult about
this elaborate page. The die cut
bows are embellished with punches. More punches are added
spilling out of the gift box, as well
as die cut balloons and a sticker.
Punches accent the journaling and
put a finishing touch on this page.

Die Cut: Ellison® Craft & Design
Font: D. J. Inkers™
Patterned Paper: Paper Patch®
Punch: McGill, Inc.
Stickers: Suzy's Zoo®
Page Designer: Kim McCrary for Pebbles In
My Pocket

*Arrange ¼″ round punches on round
template cutouts to simulate cookies.
Randomly place these embellished
cutouts around the page to reinforce the
theme of the patterned paper. Journal on
a larger template cutout.*

Patterned Paper: Paper Pizazz™ by Hot Off
The Press
Punch: McGill, Inc.
Page Designer: LeNae Gerig for Hot Off The
Press

Caleb
and
Joseph
make their favorite treat

Accent the page by using punches and reverse punches in contrasting papers to produce a patchwork effect. Make reverse punches for each corner of the page by cutting a white square and punching the center to allow the paper behind it to show.

Patterned Papers: Paper Patch®
Punch: Marvy® Uchida
Scissors: Fiskars® Paper Edgers
Sticker: Suzy's Zoo®
Computer Typeface: D. J. Inkers™
Page Designers: Kim McCrary for Pebbles In
    My Pocket

We have a very special quilt that Kaitlin asks for each time she gets sick. It is by no means beautiful, but is filled with lots of love and always makes her feel better. It was made by Grandma McCrary before she died and is pieced with scraps of all kinds. Kate never knew her Grandma McCrary but feels of her love when she cuddles in "grandma's quilt". ♥

After triple-matting the photo, place triangular corners of a contrasting paper with reverse punches as shown. Arrange four punches between the corners to form a border.

Patterned Papers: Paper Patch®
Punch: Marvy® Uchida
Scissors: Fiskars® Paper Edgers
Page Designer: Brenda Birrell for Pebbles
    In My Pocket

Mat your photos on brightly colored paper. Use corner punches on the corners of a wide mat, then cut around the punch design. Another method of using corner punches is to choose a photo with an area of vacant space in the corner. Use the corner punch on the photo and let the color of the mat behind it show through. Add stickers for a finishing touch.

Punch: Family Treasures
Stickers: ©Mrs. Grossman's Paper Co.
Page Designer: Bridgette Server for Memories & More™

Cut paper triangles to embellish the corners of the pictures. Round them and add the flowers with a corner punch. An fast, easy way to add decorative details is to color and cut out computer art.

Computer Graphics Sunflowers: D. J. Inkers™
Patterned Paper: Paper Patch®
Punches: Family Treasures
Page Designer: Brenda Birrell for Pebbles In My Pocket

WASHINGTON PARK ZOO

Our little Abby...
A simple afternoon in the sunshine... our 1 yr. old Abby is barefoot and happy to just be!!!
May 1996

Enlarge a punch with a photocopier for matching embellishments to journal on. Add details (such as the collar on the large dog) and mat the enlargements on contrasting paper. Use the original punch in the upper corners of the photo, then use a corner punch or scissors on the corresponding corners of both the photo and the mat.

Patterned Paper: Paper Patch®
Punch: Fiskars®
Scissors: Fiskars® Corner Edgers
Page Designer: Anne-Marie Spencer for Hot Off The Press

Use the method above to enlarge the sail-boat punch. Double-mat the photo, then create an L-shaped border by offsetting the page on a contrasting paper. Arrange punches around the border and add one to the enlarged sailboat.

Patterned Papers: Paper Pizazz™ by Hot Off The Press
Punch: Fiskars®
Page Designer: LeNae Gerig for Hot Off The Press

Create a lace effect on the photo mat by using decorative scissors to cut the mat, then accenting the bumps and hollows with heart and ¹⁄₁₆" circle punches. Corner scissors accent the mat and journaling plaque.

Patterned Paper: Paper Pizazz™ by Hot Off The Press
Punches: McGill, Inc.
Scissors: Fiskars® Paper Edgers and Corner Edgers
Page Designer: Kim McCrary for Pebbles In My Pocket

Lucy
Age 9

Anna
• SUMMER '96 •

To create a different effect with the lace technique, use scalloped-edged scissors and a ¹⁄₈" circle punch on a single white mat. Triple-mat on a brightly colored paper, using the widest mat for journaling.

Patterned Papers: Paper Patch®
Punch: McGill, Inc.
Scissors: Fiskars® Paper Edgers
Page Designer: Brenda Birrell for Pebbles In My Pocket

Make an elegant design by double-matting photos and using Victorian-edged scissors to create a lacy edge on the outer mats. Punch the inside of each scallop with a ¹⁄₁₆" circle punch. Accent the corners of the page and other empty spaces with stickers.

Punch: McGill, Inc.
Scissors: Fiskars® Paper Edgers
Stickers: ©Mrs. Grossman's Paper Co.
Page Designer: Kim McCrary for Pebbles In My Pocket

My Baptism Dress

Mommy made me the most beautiful white battenburg dress for my baptism. It even had a white battenburg hairbow to match. I felt like a princess wearing it. Mommy had tears in her eyes when I put it on because she said I looked like a little angel. Daddy gave me a very special gift right before we left for the Stake Center. It was a gold CTR necklace with my birthstone in it. I wore it with my beautiful new dress.

Katie's Special Day
August 6, 1994

Quaint wallpaper-type paper designs give this page a wholesome look. The offset lace-edged mat complements the effect. Use decorative scissors and a ¹⁄₈" circle punch along the edge for the lacy look.

Patterned Papers: Paper Patch®
Punch: McGill, Inc.
Scissors: Fiskars® Paper Edgers
Page Designer: Brenda Birrell for Pebbles In My Pocket

The patterned border for this page can be purchased. This is a quick and easy way to embellish a page without the work of punching, cutting and weaving the pieces yourself.

Patterned Paper: Paper Patch®
Border: Pebbles In My Pocket
Page Designer: Brenda Birrell for
Pebbles In My Pocket

Use decorative scissors and a ⅛" circle punch to make a simple lace edge that looks more complicated than it really is. Use the punch to follow the lines of the scissors. This look is really spectacular when the photos are double-matted and both mats are edged.

Patterned Paper: Paper Pizazz™ by Hot Off The
Press
Punch: McGill, Inc.
Scissors: Fiskars® Paper Edgers
Page Designer: Anne-Marie Spencer for Hot Off
The Press

Pre-cut
Archival Paper
Shapes for:
Memory & Scrap
Books
Greeting Cards
Decoration
Paper Sculpture
ACID-FREE
FADE-RESISTANT
LIGNIN FREE
FINGERPRINT-
RESISTANT
36 PAPER SHAPES
3 PAPER COLORS
CANSON
FRANCE
36 PAPER SHAPES
SELF ADHESIVE
CHRISTMAS
ARCHIVAL
CANSON
MUSEUM QUALITY
Pre-cut
Archival Paper
Shapes for:
Memory &
Scrap Books
Greeting Cards
Decoration
Paper Sculpture
ACID-FREE
FADE-RESISTANT
LIGNIN FREE
FINGERPRINT-
RESISTANT
42 PAPER SHAPES
3 PAPER COLORS
CANSON
FRANCE
42 PAPER SHAPES
Family Treasures
Die Cut Assortment
"Frames & Photo"
Spring
More than 30 Acid-Free
Shapes for Decorative Fun!
Shapes
Summer
More than 30 Acid-Free
Shapes for Decorative Fun!
Memory Book Shapes
Made in the U.S.A.

Die Cuts

Die cuts are a versatile way to add interest to your album pages. They can be used to create a background by placing them randomly all over a page, or arranged to make a scene. They can be layered around a photo to create a mat or used as a background for journaling. Many of them are available in themed packages, or as letters and words. A few are self-adhesive.

There is a wide variety of colors, but if you don't like the particular color available, simply use it as a template and trace it onto the color or pattern of paper you prefer. Many retail outlets catering to memory album customers have die-cut machines where you can create your own custom die-cut patterns to enhance your photos. Ellison® and Accu/Cut® are two companies who supply machines and dies to retailers. Here is a photo of such a machine by Ellison®.

No matter how you choose to use them, die cuts are a great way to detail an album page. And after all, it's the details that make the difference.

The borders in this section were created using a "View-lers" ruler template from Déjà Views™.

A great use for die cuts is to scatter them all over the background to make it look like a printed sheet. After arranging the die cuts, draw broken lines around the edges for a slightly more detailed look. The photos have been trimmed with a rounded corner punch.

Die Cut: Ellison® Craft & Design
Punch: Family Treasures
Page Designer: Channa Brewer for Memory Lane

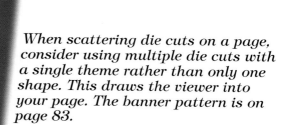

When scattering die cuts on a page, consider using multiple die cuts with a single theme rather than only one shape. This draws the viewer into your page. The banner pattern is on page 83.

Die Cut: Ellison® Craft & Design
Scissors: Fiskars® Paper Edgers
Page Designer: Anne-Marie Spencer for Hot Off The Press

Daisy...

Our Daisy came to us when she was about 9. Bonnie found her at the ball park... so abused and filthy. We cleaned her up and took her to the doctor... a $250.00 bill... we would have done anything for her because we had fallen in love with her! The girls had a group prayer and know that God had sent her to us.
xxooxo

Try layering die cuts of different patterns and sizes to give texture to a page. Let the die cuts overlap each other and even the photos where necessary.

Die Cuts: Ellison® Craft & Design
Patterned Paper: Paper Patch®
Page Designer: Brenda Birrell for Pebbles In My Pocket

Layering die cuts of different shades of green gives these leaves depth, and the tiny holes down the centers give them texture. Use the crimper to texture the trunk. The lines and dots on the coconuts create the final illusion of depth.

Corrugator: Fiskars® Paper Crimper
Die Cuts: Ellison® Craft & Design
Stickers: ©Mrs. Grossman's Paper Co.
Page Designer: Channa Brewer for Memory Lane

Maui

Richie and Jenna

Mirror the action in your photos with layered die cuts, or use them as an easy surface to journal on. Select a background paper to match the die cuts, then use a contrasting color to mat your photos.

Die Cuts: Ellison® Craft & Design
Patterned Paper: Paper Patch®
Page Designer: Anne-Marie Spencer for Hot Off The Press

™ & ©Ellison® Craft & Design

Use several of the same die cut on a page without layering, or layer only some. Using the same shape in different areas moves the eye around the page, ensuring all your photos get looked at.

Die Cuts: Ellison® Craft & Design
Patterned Paper: Paper Pizazz™ by Hot Off The Press
Scissors: Fiskars® Paper Edgers
Page Designer: Anne-Marie Spencer for Hot Off The Press

Madison is all worn out after our trip to Disneyworld

She slept all the way home in her new cap and sunglasses!

™ & ©Ellison® Craft & Design

™ & ©Ellison® Craft & Design

This page is a great example of using a die cut that coordinates with the background sheet. The tilted mat and grass add texture and break up the page, keeping the eye focused on the classic childhood picture. We like the way the grass paper was cut!

Die Cut: Ellison® Craft & Design
Patterned Paper: Paper Pizazz™ by Hot Off The Press
Page Designer: Brenda Birrell for Pebbles In My Pocket

It is easy to create a theme page when you can find die cuts, punches and paper in the same designs. Place some die cuts on the background sheet and arrange so a few overlap the mat and photo. Be sure to choose die cuts in different colors to add variety. Journal on a die cut, then add detail with various sizes of punches in complementary colors. (The large leaf patterns are on page 141.)

Die Cuts: Ellison® Craft & Design
Patterned Paper: Paper Pizazz™ by Hot Off The Press
Punches: Family Treasures
Page Designer: Ann Smith for Memory Lane

Exploring the woods w/ Dad

9-1-96

Use die cuts of different colors to create a scene. Both the hills and trees move from light to dark, creating a feeling of depth and perspective. The brown photo mats do not ruin the effect because they are a different shade from the hills. The final touch is a small campfire in the corner, complete with a stick of marshmallows running off the page. The large tree pattern is on page 82.

Die Cuts: Ellison® Craft & Design
Punch: Family Treasures
Scissors: Fiskars® Paper Edgers
Page Designer: Sharon Lewis for Memory Lane

Camping 'neath the moon and stars...

Saguaro Lake
1994

GRADE AA

If you can't think of what to do with all those small pictures, try using them with die cuts. Cut a brown paper bag and scatter die-cut fruits and vegetables across it. Crop your photos to match the shapes of the die cuts or simply insert them in empty areas. The pea pattern is on page 140.

Die Cuts: Ellison® Craft & Design
Scissors: Fiskars® Paper Edgers
Page Designer: Sandi Genovese for Ellison® Craft & Design

One of the best things about die cuts is that they are all exactly the same, so they can be used for patterns which require repeats—this checkerboard is a perfect example of this.

Die Cuts: Ellison® Craft & Design
Punch: Family Treasures
Page Designer: Sandi Genovese for Ellison® Craft & Design

This page is given a feeling of movement by tilting all the balloons in the same direction, as if they are floating away on a breeze. Another great detail on this page is the pocket at the left bottom corner which lifts up to reveal another picture. This pocket is embellished with die cuts to add interest even when the pocket is closed. The bow pattern is on page 67.

Die Cuts: Ellison® Craft & Design
Scissors: Fiskars® Paper Edgers
Stickers: Geographics Inc.
Page Designer: Sandi Genovese
for Ellison® Craft & Design

81

Die cuts represent everyday items, such as dog biscuits or footprints, but also come in more elaborate designs, such as the dog at the bottom of this page. For an unusual look, use some of the more detailed die cuts to mat your pictures.

Die Cuts: Canson®
Patterned Paper: Paper Patch®
Stencil: StenSource International, Inc.
Page Designer: Becky Goughnour for Hot Off
    The Press

To mat a photo on a die cut, lay the die cut on the photo and trace around it. Cut inside the traced line so that some of the die cut shows when the photo is glued to the center.

Die Cuts: Ellison® Craft & Design
Patterned Paper: Paper Pizazz™ by Hot Off
    The Press
Scissors: Fiskars® Paper Edgers
Page Designer: Anne-Marie Spencer for
    Hot Off The Press

Frame your photos with layers of die cuts. Center some die cuts over others, then use a pin to punch holes around each to add texture. The "super" is a die cut placed on a piece of the same paper for a neat embossed look!

Die Cuts: Ellison® Craft & Design
Scissors: Fiskars® Paper Edgers
Page Designer: Sandi Genovese for Ellison® Craft & Design

™ & ©*Ellison® Craft & Design*

Use the technique above to achieve a completely different look by piling on colors. For even more color, add stickers. The balloon patterns are on page 81.

Die Cuts: Ellison® Craft & Design
Stickers: ©Mrs. Grossman's Paper Co.
Vinyl Letters: C-Thru®
Page Designer: Sandi Genovese for Ellison® Craft & Design

™ & ©*Ellison® Craft & Design*

™ & ©*Ellison® Craft & Design*

Select plain and patterned die cuts that curve so you can wrap them around a picture as a wreath. Journal on a die-cut banner at the top. The animal patterns are on pages 140–141.

Die Cuts: Ellison® Craft & Design
Patterned Paper: Paper Patch®
Stickers: ©Mrs. Grossman's Paper Co.
Page Designer: Sandi Genovese for Ellison® Craft & Design

Die cuts placed behind the letters break up the vertical lines on this page and make the journaling easier to read. Another technique is to simply journal on the die cuts themselves.

Die Cuts: Ellison® Craft & Design
Computer Typeface: D. J. Inkers™
Patterned Papers: Paper Patch®
Page Designer: Brenda Cosgrove for Pebbles In My Pocket

™ & ©Ellison® Craft & Design

Double-mat some die cuts to hold the letters of a title. The string of popcorn and cranberries floating across the page is another excellent example of using die cuts and punches to embellish a page.

Die Cuts: Ellison® Craft & Design
Punch: McGill, Inc.
Adhesive Letters: Memory Makers
Patterned Paper: Paper Patch®
Page Designer: Brenda Cosgrove for Pebbles In My Pocket

™ & ©Ellison® Craft & Design

Die-cut shapes include letters. If you have a page with a lot of empty space, try journaling with die cuts. It is a spectacular way to tell what is going on.

Die Cuts: Ellison® Craft & Design
Patterned Paper: Paper Pizazz™ by Hot Off The Press
Punch: Marvy® Uchida
Stickers: ©Mrs. Grossman's Paper Co. and Sandylion
Scissors: Fiskars® Paper Edgers
Page Designer: Sharon Lewis for Memory Lane

TM & ©Ellison® Craft & Design

TM & © Ellison® Craft & Design

Use stickers for a page background, then journal with die-cut letters embellished with drawn dots and dashes. Add a few more die cuts in a contrasting color to balance the page.

Die Cuts: Ellison® Craft & Design
Scissors: Fiskars® Paper Edgers
Stickers: ©Mrs. Grossman's Paper Co.
Page Designer: Ann Smith for Memory Lane

TM & ©Ellison® Craft & Design

Rubber Stamping

The popularity of stamping has increased over the years. Because of the versatility, availability, and use of acid-free materials, stamping easily lends itself to the imaginative art of memory albums. The applications for stamping on photo album pages and the techniques used are varied and many. Some include: simple embellishments; creating borders; making frames and mats for photos or journaling; creating a theme; and journaling with stamps.

Standard tools and materials are acid-free pigment stamp pads, acid-free pigment markers for coloring stamps, acid-free paper and card stock, embossing powders, sticker paper, glitter, and of course...the stamps themselves! Ardent stampers will find memory albums to be an excellent outlet for their talents and a great use for their wide collections of stamps.

Have fun and experiment with different materials as you make your photo showcase uniquely yours. Some album page designers use white paper to stamp on, then cut out the images and glue them to their album pages. Others prefer to stamp on glossy sticker paper, cut out and add to their pages. Or you can stamp directly onto plain or patterned paper.

The borders for this section were created using Fiskars® Paper Edgers decorative scissors.

Create a background by randomly stamping several vegtables on a background sheet. Stamp a carrot on white paper, color with brush markers and cut out. Glue it over the corner of a photo.

Rubber Stamps: Personal Stamp Exchange
Page Designer: Julie Woolley for Paper Hearts

How Does Becky's Garden Grow?

Ian, Terina and Dia

Look Everyone...

Create a double-matted background page, then randomly stamp images that match the theme of the photos over both mats. The differences in the color and texture of the stamps add interest to the page.

Rubber Stamps: Personal Stamp Exchange
Page Designer: Stacy Julian for Paper Hearts

Use a small stamp to make a border around the page. For spectacular journaling, stamp individual letters on white paper, cut them out into ½" squares and mat the squares.

Alphabet Stamp: ©All Night Media, Inc.
Ant Stamp: Cottage Stamps
Patterned Paper: Paper Patch®
Page Designer: Julie Woolley for Paper Hearts

Create the rustic frames and banner by coloring each frame and banner stamp with two shades of the same color. Stamp and cut out the frames and use as mats for your photo. Stamp individual letters in different colors on the banner.

Patterned Paper: Paper Pizazz™ by Hot Off The Press
Rubber Stamps: Rubber Stampede®
Page Designer: Dee Gruenig for Posh Impressions

Stamp the flies with black ink, then color and cut into 1" squares. Use a black marker to make a border ⅛" from the outer edge of each square. Combine these squares with similar-sized squares of plain paper and glue randomly around the outside of the photos.

Rubber Stamps: Personal Stamp Exchange
Page Designer: Julie Woolley for Paper
    Hearts

I CAUGHT A FISH... THIS BIG!

Alternate stamping purple and violet flowers vertically from one edge of the white page to the other, being careful to alternate the stem angles as shown. Cut close to the right side of the flowers and mat the white page on a coordinating sheet of patterned paper. Stamp two extra flowers and cut out. Mount the photos as shown, draw a rectangle to journal in and place the extra stamp cutouts as shown.

Markers: Marvy® Uchida
Patterned Paper: Paper Patch®
Rubber Stamps: Rubber Stampede®
Page Designer: Julie Woolley for Paper
    Hearts

Aerobics With
Abby

Create a festive party look with colorful striped and dotted papers. Tie it all together with a stamped checkered border around the page. The dogs' party hats, the cake and the streamers are also stamped images.

Patterned Papers: Paper Patch®
Rubber Stamps: ©All Night Media, Inc.
Scissors: Fiskars® Paper Edgers
Page Designer: Barbara Barnes for All Night Media, Inc.

For a Christmas theme page, emboss Christmas balls, stars and banners with gold. Continue the theme by stamping balls strung on ribbon around the edge of the page and the row of stockings. Randomly add stamped outline stars across the page to fill any empty places.

Rubber Stamps: ©All Night Media, Inc.
Page Designer: Barbara Barnes for All Night Media, Inc.

THE BIRTHDAY BOY

What a big cake!

Great party!

THE STOCKINGS WERE HUNG BY THE CHIMNEY WITH CARE...

A VISIT FROM ST. NICK

CHRISTMAS 1996

Stamp three stage frames colored in many coordinating colors (color directly on the stamp with markers) and use to mat your photos. Place on a patterned sheet. Cut a photo to place in the foreground. Stamp a theater ticket and newspaper to use for journaling with stylized handwriting and multi-colored alphabet stamps.

Patterned Paper: Paper Pizazz™ by Hot Off The Press
Rubber Stamps: Rubber Stampede®
Page Designer: Dee Gruenig for Posh Impressions

Stamps provide a variety of interesting ways to frame your photos. Stamp a camera and film strip, then cut out the centers for an unusual mat over the photos.

Patterned Paper: Paper Pizazz™ by Hot Off The Press
Rubber Stamps: Rubber Stampede®
Page Designer: Dee Gruenig for Posh Impressions

Like many other scrapbooking items, stamps come in coordinating sets. Try using the pieces in several different ways on a page. Use a corner stamp for the bottom left photo. Use the same stamp for the frames, but add a frame stamp as well. Stamp single flowers to embellish the page and don't forget to add some shapes for journaling.

Patterned Paper: Paper Pizazz™ by Hot Off The Press
Rubber Stamps: Rubber Stampede®
Page Designer: Dee Gruenig for Posh Impressions

Dia our BIG girl.

How can you be so little and yet so grown-up?! We are so proud of you!!
Pre-school Sept. 1994

dia

meow

our cat

my house

To make an embellished frame, use black to randomly stamp on 4¾"x5" white strips, then color in and around the stamps with markers. Place the strips as shown to finish the frame. Don't forget the artwork and journaling on this fun acid-free paper.

Patterned Paper: Paper Pizazz™ by Hot Off The Press
Rubber Stamps: Whipper Snapper Designs
Page Designer: Stacy Julian for Paper Hearts

Create background paper to suit your
page with sponging. Start with the
clouds patterned sheet from Paper
Pizazz™. Place a circle template as
shown, then ink a fine make-up sponge
and lightly dab into the circle. Remove the
template to reveal the moon. Sponge darker ink for the hills. Use rubber stamps to
make the grass, tree and bats. Finally, add
your photo and journaling.

Bat Stamp: Annette Allen Watkins
Grass Stamp: Holly Pond Hill
Spider Stamp: ©All Night Media, Inc.
Tree Stamp: Peddler's Pack
Patterned Paper: Paper Pizazz™ by Hot Off The
   Press
Page Designer: Stacy Julian for Paper Hearts

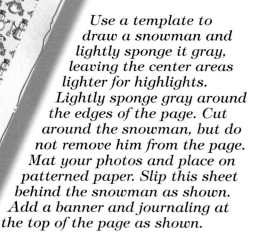

Use a template to
draw a snowman and
lightly sponge it gray,
leaving the center areas
lighter for highlights.
Lightly sponge gray around
the edges of the page. Cut
around the snowman, but do
not remove him from the page.
Mat your photos and place on
patterned paper. Slip this sheet
behind the snowman as shown.
Add a banner and journaling at
the top of the page as shown.

Patterned Paper: Paper Pizazz™ by Hot
   Off The Press
Die Cut: Ellison® Craft & Design
Template: Pebbles In My Pocket
Page Designer: Stacy Julian for Paper Hearts

Embossing is a great way to add a little texture to your stamped pages. The frames, star dust, angels and locket hearts are created with white embossing ink. The star dust is embossed directly on the page, but all the other images have been carefully cut out from another sheet of paper. The clouds are stamped on another sheet of paper and cut out.

Patterned Paper: Paper Pizazz™ by Hot Off The Press
Rubber Stamps: Rubber Stampede®
Page Designer: Dee Gruenig for Posh Impressions

Emboss the photo frames on gray paper, then cut out and use to mat your photos. Place as shown on the background sheet and use a few embossed shells on gray paper to embellish the page.

Patterned Paper: Paper Pizazz™ by Hot Off The Press
Rubber Stamps: Rubber Stampede®
Page Designer: Dee Gruenig for Posh Impressions

After matting your photos, mat a stamped image that matches the theme of the page for an elegant but simple embellishment. Notice the clever way the grass paper has been cut!

Die Cut: Ellison® Craft & Design
Patterned Papers: Paper Pizazz™ by Hot Off The Press
Rubber Stamp: Personal Stamp Exchange
Page Designer: Stacy Julian for Paper Hearts

Use a simple stamp and printed papers to provide a theme to photos where one did not exist. Use checkered paper and sunflower stamps, colored and cut out, to create a country look.

Patterned Paper: Paper Patch®
Rubber Stamp: Rubber Stampede®
Page Designer: Julie Woolley for Paper Hearts

One of the greatest features of stamping is the texture it gives an album page. The stamped and embossed fence in the foreground of the picture looks realistic, and the stamped signs look like weathered wood. The flowers, like the other stamped elements, are stamped onto a sheet of glossy sticker paper and cut out.

Patterned Paper: Paper Pizazz™ by Hot Off The Press
Rubber Stamps: Rubber Stampede®
Scissors: Fiskars® Paper Edgers
Page Designer: Dee Gruenig for Posh Impressions

Stamps can be layered to create more texture on a page. Notice the layers of grass underneath the stamped signs. This is very easy to do—simply start stamping in one shade of green and add darker shades as you move to the foreground, being careful not to overlap too much of the lighter shades.

Patterned Paper: Paper Pizazz™ by Hot Off The Press
Rubber Stamps: Rubber Stampede®
Stickers: ©Mrs. Grossman's Paper Co.
Page Designer: Dee Gruenig for Posh Impressions

ELECTRONIC CLIP ART

PROVO CRAFT

CREATIONS ON COMPUTER

ALL OCCASIONS

Designs by Annette Ward

CD-ROM

Over 200 line-art images and 1 font for use with graphic programs

Inspirations

EMILY WAS
SURPRISED
SEE THAT T
EASTER B
HAD LEFT
BA

BATH

RIDING
THE VICTORIA
ROLLER COAST
IN
POLK PARK
1995

Kaylee

Kri

PROVO

98

Decorative Extras

This chapter encompasses the extra touches and unconventional items that can be added to a page to make it unique. From computer clip art to fabrics and texturing, this is a broad category of which we've only scratched the surface here. Basically, anything can be added to a page if it meets two requirements: It must be acid-free, and it must be flat enough to slide into a sheet protector. When you take into account that anything can be copied onto acid-free paper, the possibilities are indeed endless. Of course, you can always take a photograph of a bulky item such as a corsage or bridal bouquet, enlarge it and use it as the focal point of an album page.

Would you like to display that photo of your great-grandmother with her hand-made quilt? Take a photo of the quilt, make an enlarged copy on acid-free paper and use the copy as the background sheet for your matted photos. If you are using actual fabrics in your page construction, be sure to wash them first to remove the sizing.

Rub-on letters and images are a great way to add professional-looking lettering and illustrations to your pages. They come on a transfer sheet with a protective paper underneath. When using them, cut around the images to be transferred and lay them out with the protective layer intact. Then remove the protective layer and rub the design onto your paper using a craft stick. Slowly peel back the transfer paper to reveal the design. Be sure to replace the protective sheet on the back of any unused transfers before storing them.

The border for this section was created using Fiskars® Paper Edgers decorative scissors and a punch from McGill, Inc.

One way to get design elements for your pages is to buy "cut and copy" books of clip art. You then reproduce the images with a photocopier onto white or colored paper (or even patterned paper), cut them out and glue them to your page. The two album pages on this page are great examples of lettering and decorative images from such books.

Patterned Papers: Paper Patch®
Clip Art: Little Miracles Cut & Copy by D. J. Inkers™
Page Designer: D. J. Inkers™

Patterned Papers: Paper Patch®
Clip Art: Little Miracles Cut & Copy by D. J. Inkers™
Page Designer: D. J. Inkers™

Software designed for scrapbooking can be a lot of fun—just be sure to print on acid-free and lignin-free paper. This entire page was designed on a computer.

Computer Clip Art: D. J. Inkers™
Page Designer: D. J. Inkers™

Scrapbooking software companies often offer stickers or other scrapbooking supplies to complement their programs (like these animal stickers).

Computer Clip Art: D. J. Inkers™
Patterned Papers: Paper Patch®
Stickers: D. J. Inkers™
Page Designer: D. J. Inkers™

Using scrapbooking computer software, you simply scan in your photos and place them in pre-designed page lay-outs. You can then add clip art from the software to create a theme page.

Computer Clip Art: Provo Craft® Electronic Clip Art
Stickers: Provo Craft®
Page Designer: Wes Heaps for Provo Craft®

JULY
•15•
1996

The GRAND CANYON

GONE FISHING

Look at Me!

Leah

If you don't have the equipment to scan your photos, you can design a page on your computer, print it, then place your photos. Those who don't have color printers can design their pages in black and white, then print them on colored paper, color the designs, or add stickers for color.

Computer Clip Art: Provo Craft® Electronic Clip Art
Stickers: Provo Craft®
Page Designers: Eileen Davis and Wes Heaps for Provo Craft®

EMILY WAS SURPRISED TO SEE THAT THE EASTER BUNNY HAD LEFT HER TWO BASKETS!

Use embossed frames instead of regular mats to give your pages a different look. Try offsetting them against angled background papers. Don't forget to use lots of color, too.

Embossed Frames: Memory Makers
Stickers: Frances Meyer Inc.®
Page Designer: LeNae Gerig for Hot Off The Press

Give your pages an easy touch of elegance with embossed frames. Not only is it an easy way to mat the photos, it adds texture and detail to your page. Embossed frames come in many shapes, sizes and colors to fit any photo or page.

Embossed Frame: Memory Makers
Page Designer: Bridgette Server for Memories & More™

Here's a new idea—die-cut photo corners. They wrap around the corners of your photos. Add these to your page to expand on a theme or just to add detail, as shown here. This page also makes great use of die cuts and punches to add color and interest to the page.

Photo Corners: What's New, Ltd.
Patterned Paper: Paper Pizazz™ by Hot Off The Press
Die Cuts: What's New, Ltd.
Punch: Marvy® Uchida
Page Designer: Anne-Marie Spencer for Hot Off The Press

WHETHER PLAYING IN THE BACKYARD, OR HEADING OFF TO SCHOOL

TIM THINKS BEING JOEY'S BROTHER IS THE ULTIMATE IN COOL!

The McCrary Family Christmas 1996

Christmas morning was crazy as usual. The kids slept all the way until 7 a.m. Dad and Mom were thrilled! Patrick was the official passer-outer this year so he got to wear the special Santa hat.

This deceptively simple page uses many of the best embellishments on the market. The photo corners are exciting without being overwhelming and add a great touch to this page. The background paper is accented with red and gold paper strips to make it look like a package. The white paper used for journaling has been cut like a gift tag to complete this look.

Photo Corners: What's New, Ltd.
Die Cut: Ellison® Craft & Design
Computer Typeface: D. J. Inkers™
Patterned Paper: Paper Pizazz™ by Hot Off The Press
Metallic Paper: Hygloss Products, Inc.
Page Designer: Kim McCrary for Pebbles In My Pocket

™ & ©Ellison® Craft & Design

Birthday FUN...

what a magical party!!

Kelsie with hat, wand and glitter too.

Kelsie turns 6!!

HAPPY BIRTHDAY

WARNING:
you'll have to kiss quite a few FROGS... to get a handsome prince

Princesses on Parade...

Keep in mind how pages will look facing each other in your album. The two pages shown here were designed with one theme going across both. The stripes, from patterned paper, are offset from each other so it's not important that they line up exactly. The frog and wand were rubber-stamped on another piece of paper, colored and cut out to attach to the page. What a great-looking spread!

Patterned Paper: Paper Patch®
Rubber Stamps: Inkadinkadoo
Page Designer: Stacy Julian for Paper Hearts

This elaborate page takes advantage of many great scrapbooking tools. The light purple border paper has been corrugated for texture, then punched into a lacy design. The small stickers around the edge provide a unique border that coordinates with the larger stickers and really brings the page together.

Corrugator: Fiskars® Paper Crimper
Patterned Paper: Paper Pizazz™ by Hot Off The Press
Punches: McGill, Inc.
Stickers: The Gifted Line®
Page Designer: Anne-Marie Spencer for Hot Off The Press

Strips of paper are rolled through the corrugator, then cut into "mountains." Layer corrugated strips with regular paper for extra depth. Cut around the images of the climbers and position them on the mountains. Finish with journaling and footprint punches.

Corrugator: Fiskars® Paper Crimper
Patterned Paper: Paper Pizazz™ by Hot Off The Press
Punch: Marvy® Uchida
Scissors: Fiskars® Paper Edgers
Page Designer: LeNae Gerig for Hot Off The Press

Because they are opaque, rub-ons can be overlapped to create depth in a scene. For example, the fences are plain to start with, then the signs, flowers and cat are rubbed on over them. Do not take the protective layer off the rub-on until you have decided on the placement.

Rub-ons: Provo Craft®
Page Designer: Anne-Marie Spencer for Hot Off The Press

Rub-ons provide a similar look to stickers, cutouts or computer clip art. They can be used to create a background for photos and as a framework for journaling.

Rub-ons: Provo Craft® First Impressions
Red Pen: ZIG® by EK Success Ltd.
Page Designer: Anne-Marie Spencer for Hot Off The Press

For traditional wedding photos, paper doilies can really accent the occasion. Layers of doilies in different colors and textures work well against the white satin background paper. The corner ribbon and roses were cut from another sheet of patterned paper.

Doilies: Hygloss Products, Inc.
Patterned Paper: Paper Pizazz™ by Hot Off The Press
Page Designer: Anne-Marie Spencer for Hot Off The Press

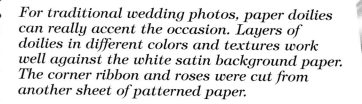

Doilies can be used for events other than weddings. This skiing page works well with the lacy doilies acting as a snow-like background.

The outer heart doily is given an extra touch by weaving acid-free ribbon along the outside and tying a bow at the top. If you have a paper doily too big to use on your page, cut it into pieces and overlap them a bit, as the designer did with the large background doily.

Doilies: Hygloss Products, Inc.
Page Designer: Anne-Marie Spencer for Hot Off The Press

Fabric torn into 1¼" strips can be loosely woven over black velour paper and glued at the edges. Crop the photos into heart shapes, mat and glue to the fabric. Cut roses out of coordinating fabric and embellish the edges of the photos with them.

Fabric: V. I. P.® Fabrics
Velour Paper: Hygloss Products, Inc.
Page Designer: Anne-Marie Spencer for Hot Off The Press

Kevin learning to feed himself for the first time. What a smart baby!

Cover a rectangle of card-stock paper with fabric, then cover inexpensive photo mats with coordinating fabric and use to mat photos and a journaling shape. Be sure to launder the fabric to remove any sizing.

Fabric: V. I. P.® Fabrics
Page Designer: Anne-Marie Spencer for Hot Off The Press

110

Journaling

The final touch to your memory album page is journaling, which provides the information needed to fully appreciate and understand the photos. Plan the journaling space before the work on a page begins. The extent and style of journaling may vary according to the nature of the photos (such as formal or informal), the paper and tools available, and your own comfort level. It can be as simple or as complicated as you want it to be.

Leave adequate space—maybe even reduce the number of photos. Decide whether you will write on the background paper, template cutouts, die cuts, photo mats, simple plaques, or the page border. Remember that writing on patterned or dark paper may require different techniques and tools. Rub-on letters may not show up on dark or patterned paper. Colored papers might need contrasting, metallic or white ink. Bold lettering with a broad-tip pen may be necessary on patterned paper. Sticker letters are more effective if they coordinate with other items on a page. You may prefer to use a computer for journaling.

Archival journaling is your opportunity to chronicle important events and ancestors in your family history that might otherwise be forgotten; it's often more structured than the storylines accompanying everyday snapshots. Be creative and have fun when journaling informal photos. Describe details of Baby's first step, Grandma's birthday party or cousin John's wedding that will be satisfying to reflect on in years to come. Don't hesitate to add personalality and humor. Your perspective gives insights to future generations!

To ensure permanency and to prevent damage to your treasured photos, use only acid-free photo-safe pens. It's fun to try a wide selection of pen styles and colors. Let your personality show through your photo journaling efforts. Don't worry about your handwriting (most people dislike theirs!)—the most important thing is to get the information down on paper. Ability and comfort will naturally increase as you develop your own style.

The borders for this section were created using Fiskars®
Paper Edgers decorative scissors.

Rub-on details make this page so easy! The cats, birdhouse and lettering are rub-ons, while the house (pattern on page 140) is made of paper and trimmed with patterned strips.

Patterned Papers: MPR Paperbilities™ and Paper Pizazz™ by Hot Off The Press
Rub-ons: True Expressions™ Magic Memories from Chartpak®
Page Designer: Anne-Marie Spencer for Hot Off The Press

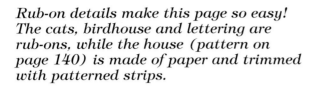

The tea party rub-ons repeat the theme of the photos. The journaling phrase comes on a sheet with the tea party images.

Patterned Paper: Paper Patch®
Rub-ons: True Expressions™ Magic Memories from Chartpak®
Scissors: Fiskars® Paper Edgers
Page Designer: Anne-Marie Spencer for Hot Off The Press

Letter stickers with a floral look carry the garden theme from the photos onto the page. Matching flower stickers in the center and bottom corners balance the page and make the large stickers look more natural.

Scissors: Fiskars® Paper Edgers
Stickers: Frances Meyer, Inc.®
Page Designer: Anne-Marie Spencer for Hot Off The Press

Stickers are used not only for the title and date, but also to make a colored border along two sides of the page.

Scissors: Fiskars® Paper Edgers
Stickers: ©Mrs. Grossman's Paper Co.
Page Designer: Anne-Marie Spencer for Hot Off The Press

ABCDEFGHIJK
LMNOPQRSTUV
WXYZ

abcdefghijklm
nopqrstuvwxyz

1234567890

Primary colors and chunky lettering complement the child's play theme of this page. Wide mats around the photos and a wide page border provide ample room for journaling.

Patterned Paper: Paper Pizazz™ by Hot Off The Press
Scissors: Fiskars® Paper Edgers
Small Hand Punch: McGill, Inc.
Large Hand Template: Provo Craft®
Page Designer: LeNae Gerig for Hot Off The Press
Lettering: Becky Goughnour for Hot Off The Press

ABCDEFGHIJ
KLMNOPQRS
TUVWXYZ ab
cdefghijklmn
opqrstuvwx
yz 12
3456
7890

Journal around the subjects for a striking storyline effect. The folksy outline lettering is perfect for a page packed with activity. The small water drop was cut from a template, then traced slightly larger to make the other drop.

Patterned Paper: Paper Pizazz™ by Hot Off The Press
Water Drop Template: Extra Special Products
Page Designer: Becky Goughnour for Hot Off The Press

ABCDEF
GHIJKLM
NOPQRST
UVWXYZ
ABCDEFGHI
JKLMNOPQR
STUVWXYZ
1234567890

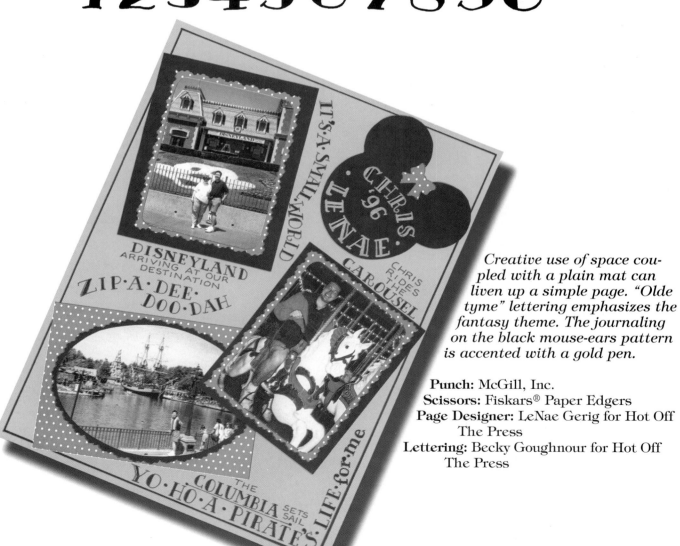

Creative use of space coupled with a plain mat can liven up a simple page. "Olde tyme" lettering emphasizes the fantasy theme. The journaling on the black mouse-ears pattern is accented with a gold pen.

Punch: McGill, Inc.
Scissors: Fiskars® Paper Edgers
Page Designer: LeNae Gerig for Hot Off The Press
Lettering: Becky Goughnour for Hot Off The Press

ABCDEFGHIJKLM
NOPQRSTUVWXYZ
abcdefghijklmnopqr
stuvwxyz1234567890

ABCDEFGHIJKLMN
OPQRSTUVWXYZ
abcdefghijklmnopqrst
uvwxyz1234567890

Adding ball or stick accents to plain block lettering is easy to do and adds a decorative touch. The journaling on this album page is triple matted to call attention to it. A brief explanation of the action enhances the appreciation of the photo. The cloud patterns are on page 141.

Patterned Papers: Paper Patch® and Paper Pizazz™ by Hot Off The Press
Scissors: Fiskars® Paper Edgers
Punch: Family Treasures™
Die Cuts: Ellison® Craft & Design
Stickers: ©Mrs. Grossman's Paper Co.
Page Designer: Kim McCrary for Pebbles In My Pocket
Lettering: Becky Goughnour for Hot Off The Press

ABCDEFGHIJKLMN
OPQRSTUVWXYZ
abcdefghijklmnopqrst
uvwxyz 1234567890

Rope lettering adds to the nautical appeal of this page. The title was lettered on white paper, then cut out and matted. Die cuts are useful for journaling as well as embellishments.

Die Cuts: Canson®
Scissors: Fiskars® Paper Edgers
Stickers: ©Mrs. Grossman's Sticker Co.
Page Designer: Bridgette Server for Memories & More™
Lettering: Becky Goughnour for Hot Off The Press

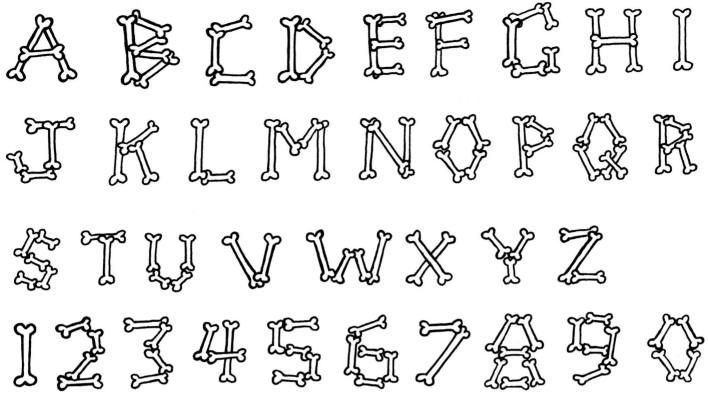

The "bones" lettering is perfect for this Halloween page, but would also be great for a doggie page. The skeleton stickers reinforce the Halloween theme and add pizazz to a plain black background.

Patterned Paper: Paper Patch®
Scissors: Family Treasures™
Stickers: ©Mrs. Grossman's Paper Co.
Page Designer: Monica Schmidt for Memory Lane
Lettering: Becky Goughnour for Hot Off The Press

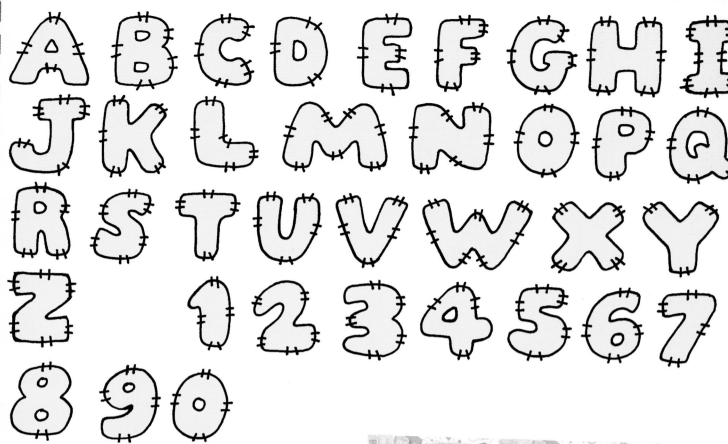

Combine styles and sizes of lettering to create page interest. The puffy "stitched" look of the title lettering adds a comfy quilt look to the page. Stickers add excitement to empty space, accent photos and frame journaling.

Pattered Paper: Paper Pizazz™ by Hot Off The Press
Scissors: Fiskars® Paper Edgers
Stickers: Frances Meyer Inc.®
Page Designer: Anne-Marie Spencer for Hot Off The Press
Lettering: Becky Goughnour for Hot Off The Press

A B C D E F G H I J K L M
N O P Q R S T U V W X Y Z
a b c d e f g h i j k l m n
o p q r s t u v w x y z
1 2 3 4 5 6 7 8 9 0

Elegant calligraphy combines with pearls, paper lace doilies and satiny trim to make a page as pretty as a picture. Layering of elements creates a three-dimensional look.

Doilies: HyGloss Products, Inc.
Patterned Paper: Paper Pizazz™ by Hot Off The Press
Pearls, Gimp Braid: Wm. E. Wright
Scissors: Fiskars® Paper Edgers
Page Designer: Anne-Marie Spencer for Hot Off The Press
Lettering: Becky Goughnour for Hot Off The Press

Keepsake Items

Chances are you have precious letters, children's art-work or newspaper clippings tucked away in the back of a drawer or closet, much like those old boxes of photos! A wonderful way to preserve these special mementos is to combine them with related photos on a page in your memory album.

In the following chapter, we've given you some ideas to get you started, but don't be limited—let your imagination be your guide. A good report card, schoolwork samples and awards of recognition are just a few of the items upon which you can build a theme page. Just keep in mind that most of these things will not be acid-free, so be sure to color photo-copy them onto acid-free paper. A color copy will also allow you to use a dimensional item like a graduation tassel or a medal, as illustrated on page 127.

With just a little creativity, you can turn these pre-cious items into treasured album pages to give even more personality to your albums.

The border in this section was created using Fiskars® Paper Edgers decorative scissors.

Making an acid-free color copy is a wonderful way to preserve a child's letters or artwork. You can reduce the pieces to fit the page, then add photos of the child. Don't forget to include journaling with the artist's name and age.

Scissors: Fiskars® Paper Edgers
Page Designer: LeNae Gerig for Hot Off The Press

Kids can join in the scrapbooking fun! Encourage kids to make and autograph acid-free paper works of art, then mat their photographs right on the page.

Scissors: Fiskars® Paper Edgers
Page Designer: LeNae Gerig for Hot Off The Press

Tickets and action photographs combine to make this page a real splash! The matching stickers are eye-catching, they match the photo and they are a great way to tie a page together.

Scissors: Fiskars® Paper Edgers
Ruler: Déjà Views™ by C-Thru®
Stickers: Frances Meyer Inc.®
Page Designer: LeNae Gerig for Hot Off The Press

Make a pocket by fastening the side and bottom edges of sheet music to the base sheet of paper, then tuck in souvenir tickets and a playbill. Stencils and stickers add pizazz.

Stencil: Déjà Views™ by C-Thru®
Die cuts: Ellison® Craft & Design
Stickers: ©Mrs. Grossman's Paper Company
Page Designer: Sandi Genovese for Ellison® Craft & Design

Pressed flowers from the bride's bouquet add a romantic touch to this beautiful announcement and photo page.

Paper: Paper Pizazz™ by Hot Off The Press
Scissors: Fiskars® Paper Edgers
Page Designer: LeNae Gerig for Hot Off The Press

Mat a senior portrait and name card on matching paper, then add a graduation announcement to make an easy graduation keepsake.

Paper: Paper Pizazz™ by Hot Off The Press
Page Designer: LeNae Gerig for Hot Off The Press

Make an acid-free color copy of a ribbon or use the actual ribbon to create a unique page that showcases talent and achievement. (The piano key pattern is on page 142.)

Patterned Paper: Paper Pizazz™ by Hot Off The Press
Scissors: Fiskars® Paper Edgers
Stickers: Frances Meyer Inc.®
Page Designer: Becky Goughnour for Hot Off The Press

Place a medal directly onto a color photocopier to make an acid-free background page with shadows that complement the team photograph.

Scissors: Fiskars® Paper Edgers
Page Designer: LeNae Gerig for Hot Off The Press

School awards and newspaper articles copied onto acid-free paper make a great start to an impressive page (do not place newspaper articles directly into your album, because newsprint contains lignin). Complete the effect with portraits of the successful student.

Paper: Paper Pizazz® by Hot Off The Press
Scissors: Fiskars® Paper Edgers
Page Designer: LeNae Gerig for Hot Off The Press

This souvenir Navy "certificate" is copied onto acid-free paper and reduced in size to create a fun centerpiece for the page. Surround the certificate with photos on matching mats and use stencils to create the anchors and rope border.

Stencil: StenSource International, Inc.
Page Designer: Anne-Marie Spencer for Hot Off The Press

When you have many newspaper articles about one event, copy them onto acid-free paper and reduce them in size to provide the background for a photo. Fleur-de-lis punched in the corners of the photo and glued to the background paper corners add a polished touch.

Paper: Paper Pizazz™ by Hot Off The Press
Punch: Family Treasures
Page Designer: Anne-Marie Spencer for Hot Off The Press

Create a beautiful graduation page by making an acid-free photocopy of the diploma, then mounting the graduation photo behind an embossed mat. Hand-drawn ivy leaves form the border.

Metallic Paper: Hygloss Products, Inc.
Scissors: Fiskars® Paper Edgers
Embossed Mat: Making Memories
Page Designer: Becky Goughnour for Hot Off The Press

Mat a postcard for the centerpiece of the page, then surround it with candid photographs from the visit. To be sure the postcard is acid-free, check it with a pH tester pen, or just make a color photocopy of it.

Paper: Paper Pizazz™ by Hot Off The Press
Scissors: Fiskars® Paper Edgers
Page Designer: Anne-Marie Spencer for Hot Off The Press

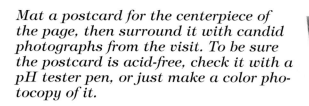

Multnomah Falls

Ice cream at Multnomah Falls. No sooner did we buy our cones than the sun disappeared and a bitter wind and rain took its place.

Combine a postcard with close-up photographs to create a striking page. A die cut and banner make interesting journaling pieces.

Textured Paper: Hygloss Products, Inc.
Patterned Paper: Paper Pizazz™ by Hot Off The Press
Scissors: Fiskars® Paper Edgers
Ruler: Déjà Views™ by C-Thru®
Die cut: Ellison® Craft & Design
Page Designer: Becky Goughnour for Hot Off The Press

Create a pocket with a Victorian card, then tuck in an antique handkerchief and other Victorian items.

Stickers: The Gifted Line®
Scissors: Fiskars® Paper Edgers
Page Designer: Anne Cook for The Gifted Line®

To make an envelope for the hair from a child's first haircut: Cut the corner of a sheet protector, then glue one open side closed and trim the top edge for a flap, as shown in the diagram.

Paper: Paper Patch®
Scissors: Fiskars® Paper Edgers
Die Cut: Canson®
Stickers: ©Mrs. Grossman's Paper Company
Page Designer: LeNae Gerig for Hot Off The Press

trim away gray areas on back flap and entire front flap

leave open

glue

Black & White Photos

Black-and-white photos can be one of the greatest challenges to memory album crafters. They are generally the only copies of your oldest photos and, with no existing negatives, you may be hesitant to cut them.

The best way to avoid "scissor regret" is to make acid-free photocopies of the photos and use them to lay out your page design. By so doing, cutting mistakes can be corrected easily by simply throwing away or recutting the copy until you are satisfied with the presentation. (If you are going to use the copy in the final page, rather than the original, we recommend using a color copier, as it will pick up the subtle shadings of the photo better than a black-and-white copier.)

Another consideration must be given to the colors of the background papers, which in the past may have seemed overwhelming or uncomplimentary when paired with the sepia browns or grays found in monochrome photographs. Today, publishers are becoming aware of the need for acid-free paper to complement these photos.

Another option for creating interest with black and white photos is hand-coloring the photographs with a product like Delta's SoftTints™ (found in craft stores). Combine one part paint with two parts Delta Color Float™ and use a brush to lightly color the chosen areas of the photograph. You can go for a minimal effect, adding a soft tint to cheeks and lips, or an all-over look, coloring the entire photo. Pastels are achieved by adding a small amount of white to the paint mix. Check the color on scrap paper before applying it to the photo. Again, a color copy of the photo makes a great canvas for experimentation. This technique looks best on true black-and-white photos and is not recommended for sepia or gold-tone photographs.

The borders in this section were created using Fiskars® Paper Edgers decorative scissors.

133

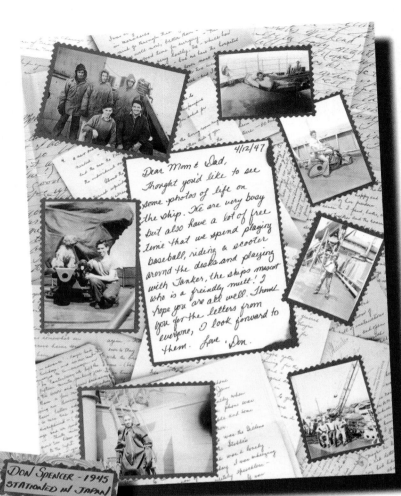

A keepsake letter and old photographs make this page a treasure. The letter-patterned paper ties the theme together.

Patterned Paper: Paper Pizazz™ by Hot Off The Press
Scissors: Fiskars® Paper Edgers
Page Designer: Anne-Marie Spencer for Hot Off The Press

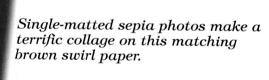

Single-matted sepia photos make a terrific collage on this matching brown swirl paper.

Patterned Paper: Paper Pizazz™ by Hot Off The Press
Scissors: Fiskars® Paper Edgers
Page Designer: Anne-Marie Spencer for Hot Off The Press

Trace the stencil onto opposite corners, then cut out with an X-acto® knife and mount on metallic paper. Mat the journaling with matching paper.

Metallic and Velour Papers: Hygloss Products Inc.
Scissors: Fiskars® Paper Edgers
Stencils: StenSource International, Inc.
Page Designer: Anne-Marie Spencer for Hot Off The Press

The wedding of Dorothy V. Price to William N. White, Aug 9, 1947

1950

1961

Sylvia's Gallery

1952

1962

Tie sepia photographs together with black-and-white ones by using brown and grey frames over a neutral paper. The corners were cut with special scissors.

Patterned Papers: Paper Pizazz™ by Hot Off The Press
Scissors: Fiskars® Corner Edgers
Page Designer: Anne-Marie Spencer for Hot Off The Press

Black-and-white photos can work with colored paper! Make a pattern from plain paper to match the theme of your page. (The ship pattern is on page 142.)

Patterned Paper: Paper Pizazz™ by Hot Off the Press
Scissors: Fiskars® Paper Edgers
Page Designer: Anne-Marie Spencer for Hot Off The Press

A regal photograph is made even more elegant with embellishments and metallic paper. Choose finishing touches like these metallic paper charms and cut-apart metallic doilies to accentuate a single photo on a page.

Patterned Paper: Paper Pizazz™ by Hot Off The Press
Velour Paper: Hygloss Products, Inc.
Doily: Hygloss Products, Inc.
Punch: McGill, Inc.
Page Designer: Anne-Marie Spencer for Hot Off The Press

Use stickers to embellish a page of black-and-white mixed with color photos.

Stickers: The Gifted Line®
Scissors: Fiskars® Paper Edgers
Page Designer: Anne Cook for The Gifted Line®

Bill and Yvonne

Weddings of 1954

Ken and Jean

Alan and Joyce

Matting not just the individual photographs, but the entire page creates an especially lovely three-dimensional look.

Patterned Paper: Paper Pizazz™ by Hot Off The Press
Scissors: Fiskars® Paper Edgers and Corner Edgers
Stickers: Frances Meyer Inc.®
Page Designer: Anne-Marie Spencer for Hot Off The Press

Triple matting, layered corners and decorative punches all emphasize this hand-tinted sepia photograph.

Patterned Paper: Paper Patch®
Scissors: Fiskars® Paper Edgers and Corner Edgers
Punch: Marvy® Uchida
Page Designer: LeNae Gerig for Hot Off The Press

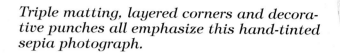

This hand-tinted sepia photograph is emphasized by heart-shaped paper doilies and complementary paper colors.

Doilies: Hygloss Products, Inc.
Scissors: Family Treasures
Page Designer: Anne-Marie Spencer for Hot Off The Press

Small hand-tinted photographs on filmstrip paper create an old fashioned look that's a "reel" pleaser!

Patterned Paper: Paper Pizazz™ by Hot Off The Press
Scissors: Fiskars® Paper Edgers
Page Designer: Anne-Marie Spencer for Hot Off The Press

Emphasize vivid hand-tinted photographs by adding matching paper and using stickers that accentuate the theme.

Scissors: Fiskars® Paper Edgers
Stickers: Mary Engelbreit® for Melissa Neufeld, Inc.
Page Designer: Anne-Marie Spencer for Hot Off The Press

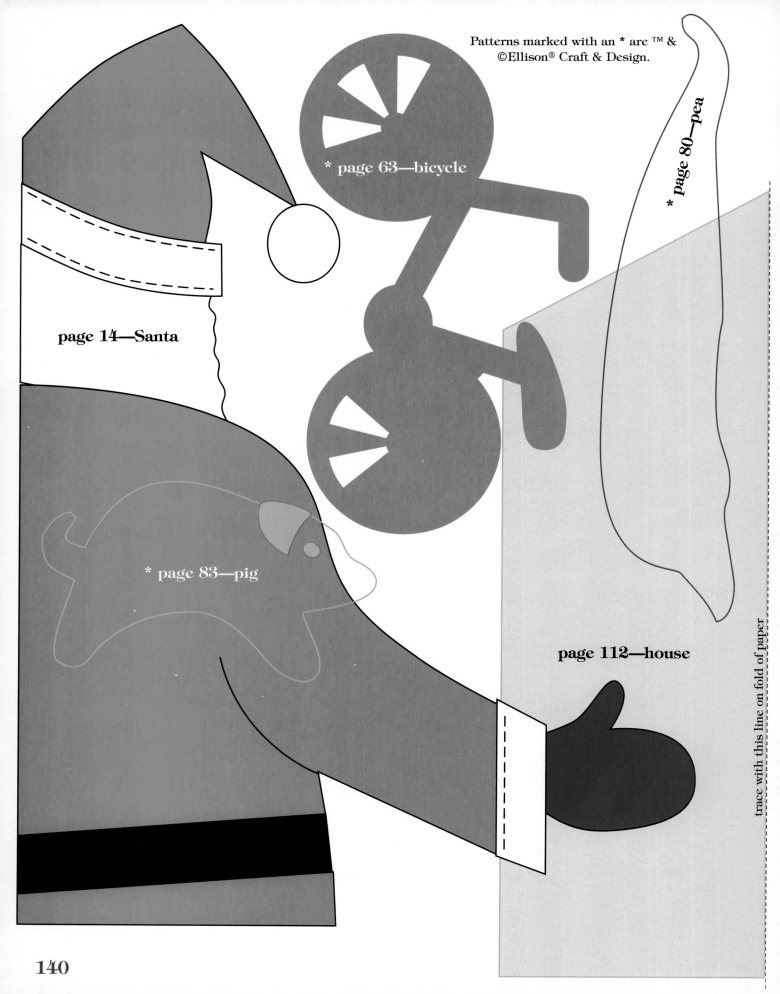

Patterns marked with an * are ™ &
©Ellison® Craft & Design.

* page 63—bicycle

* page 80—pea

page 14—Santa

* page 83—pig

page 112—house

trace with this line on fold of paper

140

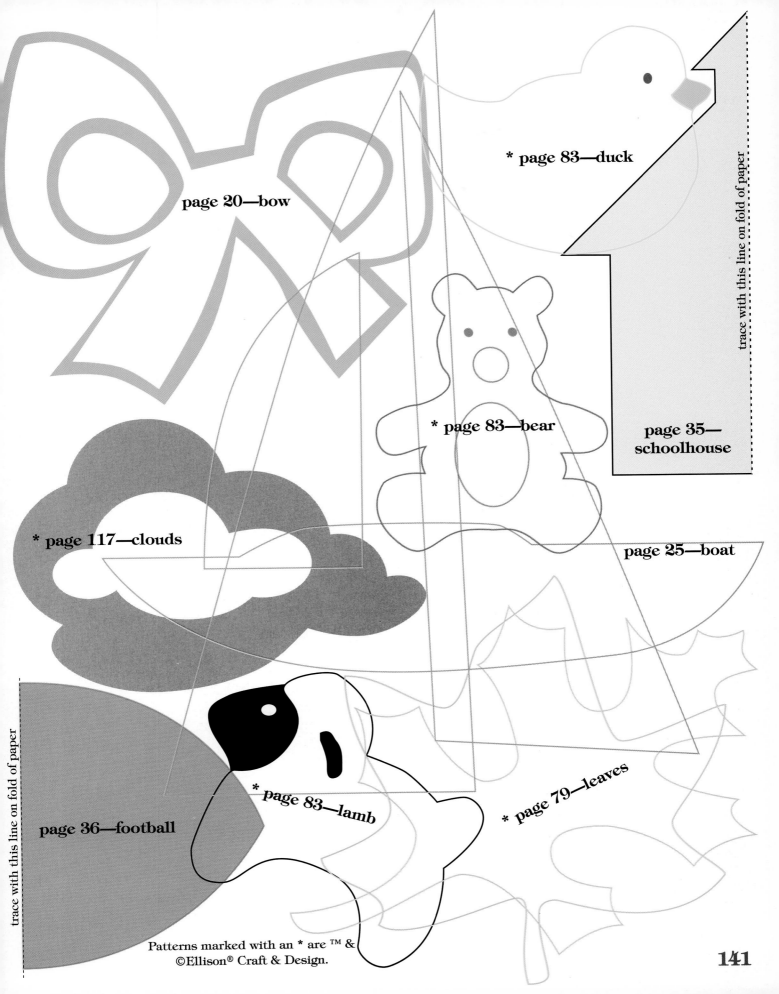

* page 83—duck

page 20—bow

trace with this line on fold of paper

page 35—
schoolhouse

* page 83—bear

* page 117—clouds

page 25—boat

trace with this line on fold of paper

* page 83—lamb

* page 79—leaves

page 36—football

Patterns marked with an * are ™ &
©Ellison® Craft & Design.

141

page 41—pizza slice

page 136—ship

trace with this line on fold of paper

page 41—hamburger

Acid-free
Acid is used in paper manufacturing to break apart the wood fibers and the lignin which holds them together. If acid remains in the materials used for photo albums, the acid can react chemically with photographs and accelerate their deterioration. Acid-free products have a pH factor of 7 to 8.5. It's imperative that all materials (glue, pens, paper, etc.) used in memory albums or scrapbooks be acid-free.

Acid migration
is the transfer of acidity from one item to another through physical contact or acidic vapors. If a newspaper clipping were put into an album, the area it touched would turn yellow or brown. A de-acidification spray can be used on acidic papers, or they can be color copied onto acid-free papers.

Archival quality
is a term used to indicate materials which have undergone laboratory analysis to determine their acidic and buffered content.

Buffered Paper
During manufacture a buffering agent such as calcium carbonate or magnesium bicarbonate can be added to paper to neutralize acid contaminants. Such papers have a pH of 8.5.

Cropping
Cutting or trimming a photo to keep only the most important parts. See page 11 for cropping ideas and information about cropping Polaroid photos.

Imprintables
A term used in the stationery market for papers which have a plain center and a design on the border. With the center empty, the paper can be printed on for party invitations or announcements.

Journaling
refers to the text on an album page giving details about the photographs. Journaling can be done in your own handwriting or with adhesive letters, rub-ons, etc. It is probably the most important part of memory albums. See pages 110-121 for more information.

Lignin
is the bonding material which holds wood fibers together as a tree grows. If lignin remains in the final paper product (as with newsprint) it will become yellow and brittle over time. Most paper other than newsprint is lignin-free.

pH factor
refers to the acidity of a paper. The pH scale is the standard for measurement of acidity and alkalinity. It runs from 0 to 14 with each number representing a ten-fold increase; pH neutral is 7. Acid-free products have a pH factor from 7 to 8.5. Special pH tester pens are available to help you determine the acidity or alkalinity of products.

Photo-safe
is a term similar to archival quality but more specific to materials used with photographs. Acid-free is the determining factor for a product to be labeled photo-safe.

Sheet protectors
These are made of plastic to slip over a finished album page. They can be side-loading or top-loading and fit 8½"x11" pages or 12"x12" sheets. It is important that they be acid-free. Polypropylene is commonly used—never use vinyl sheet protectors.

Sources

Manufacturers & Suppliers

Accu/Cut® Systems
1035 E. Dodge St.
Fremont, NE 68025

Acme United Corporation
75 Kings Hwy Cutoff
Fairfield, CT 06430

All Night Media, Inc.
Post Office Box 10607
San Rafael, CA 94912

Boston International, Inc.
94 Rowe St.
Newton, MA 02166

Canson-Talens, Inc.
21 Industrial Dr.
S. Hadley, MA 01075

Chartpak®
One River Road
Leeds, MA 01053

Cottage Stamps
533 Lower Sunnyslope Rd.
Wenatchee, WA 98801

D. J. Inkers™
Post Office Box 2462
Sandy, UT 84091

D.O.T.S.™
738 East Quality Dr
American Fork, UT 84003

Déjà Views™ by C-Thru®
6 Britton Dr.
Bloomfield, CT 06002

EK Success Ltd.
611 Industrial Rd.
Carlstadt, NJ 07072

Ellison Craft & Design
Toll Free 888-972-7238
714-724-0555

Extra Special Products Corp.
Post Office Box 777
Greenville, OH 45331

Family Treasures, Inc.
24922 Anza Dr., Unit D
Valencia, CA 91355

Fiskars Inc.
7811 W. Stewart Avenue
Wausau, WI 54401

Frances Meyer Inc.®
Post Office Box 3088
Savannah, GA 31402

Geographics, Inc.
Post Office Box 1750
Blaine, WA 98230

Gussie's
Post Office Box 181179
Dallas, TX 75218

Holly Pond Hill
132 W. Mountain Ave.
Fort Collins, CO 80524

Hot Off The Press
1250 NW Third, Dept LA
Canby, OR 97013

Hygloss Products, Inc.
402 Broadway
Passaic, NJ 07055

Inkadinkadoo, Inc.
60 Cummings Park
Woburn, MA 01801

Making Memories
Post Office Box 1188
Centerville, UT 84014

Mara-Mi, Inc.
650 Taft Street, NE
Minneapolis, MN 55413

Marvy® Uchida
3535 Del Amo Blvd
Torrance, CA 90503

McGill, Inc.
Post Office Box 177
Marengo, IL 60152

Melissa Neufeld Inc.
6940 Koll Center Parkway, Suite 100
Pleasanton, CA 94566

**Mounting Memories Keepsake
  Glue by Beacon™**
Post Office Box 427
Wyckoff, NJ 07481

MPR Associates, Inc.
529 Townsend Avenue
High Point, NC 27263

Mrs. Grossman's Paper Company
Post Office Box 4467
Petaluma, CA 94955

Peddler's Pack
4570 SW Watson
Beaverton, OR 97005

Personal Stamp Exchange
360 Sutton Place
Santa Rosa, CA 95407

Provo Craft®
285 E. 900 South
Provo, UT 84606

Rubber Stampede®
Post Office Box 246
Berkeley, CA 94701

Sonburn
Post Office Box 167
Addison, TX 75001

StenSource International, Inc.
18971 Hess Avenue
Sonora, CA 95370

Stickopotamus™
611 Industrial Rd.
Carlstadt, NJ 07072

Suzy's Zoo
9401 Waples St.
San Diego, CA 92121

The Gifted Line®
1-800-5-GIFTED
FAX 510-215-4772

The Paper Patch
Post Office Box 414
Riverton, UT 84065

What's New Ltd.
3716 E. Main St.
Mesa, AZ 85205

Whipper Snapper Designs
1837 S. Nevada Ave. #247
Colorado Springs, CO 80906

Z-Barten Productions
8611 Hayden Pl.
Culver City, CA 90232

Retail Stores:

Memories & More™
CA, UT, CO, NV
1-800-286-5263

Memory Lane
700 E. Southern Avenue
Mesa, AZ 85204

Paper Hearts
6185 Highland Dr.
Salt Lake City, UT 84121

Pebbles In My Pocket
1132 S. State St.
Orem, UT 84058

Posh Impressions
4708 Barranca Parkway
Irvine, CA 92604

The borders in this section were created
with a corner punch from Family Treasures.